Pocket Rough Guide

PRAGUE

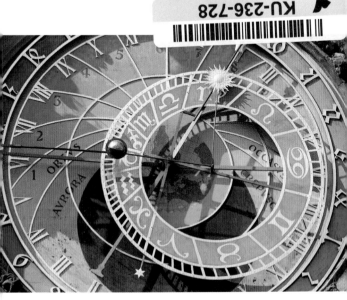

this third edition updated by

MARC DI DUCA

Contents

INTRODUCTION TO
PRAGUE

With some six hundred years of architecture virtually untouched by natural disaster or war, few other European capitals look quite as beautiful as Prague. Straddling the winding River Vltava, with a steep wooded hill to one side, the city retains much of its medieval layout, and its rich mantle of Baroque, Rococo and Art Nouveau buildings have successfully escaped the vanities and excesses of modern redevelopment.

BUILDINGS ON THE OLD TOWN SQUARE

Best place for a view over the city

Prague is a city of red rooftops and golden spires, of wooded hills and stupendous views. Every visitor who climbs the steps to the castle is rewarded with a fantastic view over the city, but if you want to escape the crowds, check out some of the capital's other lofty vantage points.
See Letná > p.118, Petřín > p.54, Vyšehrad > p.110.

Physically, Prague may have weathered the twentieth century very well but it suffered in other ways. The city that produced the music of Dvořák and Smetana, the literature of Čapek and Kafka and modernist architecture to rival Bauhaus, was forced to endure a brutal Nazi occupation. Prague had always been a multiethnic city, with a large Jewish and German-speaking population – in the aftermath of the war, only the Czechs were left. Then for forty years, during the Communist period, the city lay hidden behind the Iron Curtain, seldom visited by Westerners. All that changed in the 1990s, and nowadays Prague is one of the most popular European city break destinations, with a highly developed tourist industry and a large expat population who,

if nothing else, help to boost the city's nightlife.

Prague is divided into two unequal halves by the river, which meanders through the heart of the capital and provides the city with one of its most enduring landmarks, Charles Bridge. Built during the city's medieval golden age, this stone bridge, with its parade of Baroque statuary, still forms the chief link between the more central old town, or Staré Město, on the right bank, and Prague's hilltop castle on the left. The castle is a vast complex, which towers over the rest of the city and supplies the classic picture-postcard image of Prague. Spread across the slopes below the castle are the wonderful cobbled streets and secret walled gardens of Malá Strana, little changed in the two hundred years since Mozart walked them.

When to visit

Prague is very popular, which means that the streets around the main sights are jam-packed with tourists for much of the year. If you can, it's best to avoid the summer months, when temperatures sometimes soar above 30°C, and you have to fight your way across Charles Bridge. The best times to visit, in terms of weather, are May and September. The winter months can be very chilly in Prague, but if you don't mind the cold, the city does look good in the snow and the crowds are manageable. Christmas and New Year are perfect as there are Christmas markets right across town, and plenty of mulled wine and hot punch to keep you warm.

With a population of just one and a quarter million, Prague (Praha to the Czechs) is relatively small as capital cities go. It originally developed as four separate self-governing towns and a Jewish ghetto, whose individual identities and medieval street plans have been preserved, to a greater or lesser extent, to this day. Almost everything of any historical interest lies within these compact central districts, and despite the twisting matrix of streets, it's easy enough to find your way around between the major landmarks. If you do use public transport, you'll find an extensive and picturesque tram network and a futuristic Soviet-built metro system that rivals most German cities. Price rises over the last decade mean Prague is no longer the budget destination it once was. However, one thing you can be sure of is that the beer is better and cheaper than anywhere else in the EU.

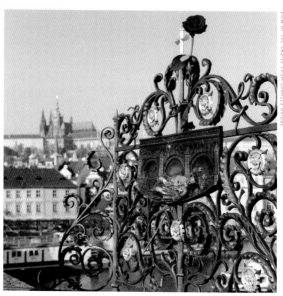

VIEW OF THE CASTLE FROM CHARLES BRIDGE

PRAGUE AT A GLANCE

>> EATING

As in many cities, the main thoroughfares in Prague aren't the best places in which to find somewhere to eat and drink. One or two grand Habsburg-era cafés survive on the main junctions of the city centre, but for the most part the best cafés and restaurants are hidden away in the backstreets. There's a particularly acute dearth of decent places in and around Prague Castle and **Hradčany**, while expensive restaurants predominate in **Malá Strana**. For a much wider choice of cafés, and of cuisine, head to **Staré Město** and the streets of **Nové Město** just south of Národní.

>> DRINKING

Given that the Czechs top the world league table of beer consumption, it comes as little surprise to find that Prague is a drinker's paradise. Wherever you are in the city, you're never very far from a pub or bar where you can quench your thirst. **Staré Město** has the highest concentration of pubs and bars, but if you're looking for one of the city's new microbreweries or for a traditional Czech pub (**pivnice**), you'll need to explore the residential streets of **Nové Město**, **Vinohrady** or **Holešovice**. Look out, too, for the many alfresco drinking spots beside the river, on one of the islands, or in one of the city's many public parks.

>> NIGHTLIFE

Prague's often excellent theatre and concert venues are all very centrally located in **Staré Město** and **Nové Město**; the same is true for most small and medium-scale jazz and rock venues. **Žižkov** has more late-night pubs and bars than anywhere else, plus a smattering of gay and lesbian venues. One area that's up-and-coming for nightlife is **Holešovice**, in particular the old industrial and market area to the east of the metro line – the warehouse spaces here already house several of the city's newest clubs and venues. **Wenceslas Square** remains the traditional centre of Prague's seedier side.

>> SHOPPING

Pařížská, in Josefov, is home to the city's swankiest stores, among them branches of the international fashion houses. Celetná in Staré Město, and Na příkopě on the border of Nové Město, also specialize in luxury goods. The city's most modern department store is multistorey My národní on Národní. Czechs have had their own malls – known as *pasáže* – since the 1920s, and new ones continue to sprout up. The mother of all malls is Palladium, on Náměstí Republiky, housed in a castellated former army barracks. For more offbeat, independent shops you need to explore the cobbled side streets of Staré Město and Nové Město.

OUR RECOMMENDATIONS FOR WHERE TO EAT, DRINK AND SHOP ARE LISTED AT THE END OF EACH PLACES CHAPTER.

Day One in Prague

1 Prague Castle > p.32. From Hradčanské naměstí, the square outside the main castle gates, you get an incredible view over Prague.

2 Cathedral of sv Víta > p.32. Occupying centre stage in the castle's vast precincts is the city's Gothic cathedral.

3 Old Royal Palace > p.35. Visit the palace's vast, rib-vaulted Vladislav Hall.

4 Golden Lane > p.37. Built in the sixteenth century for the imperial guards, these tiny little cottages situated hard against the fortifications are now one of the most popular sights in the castle.

Lunch > p.39. *Villa Richter*, situated in the middle of the castle vineyards, has superb views across the rooftops and river to Staré Město.

5 Church of sv Mikuláš > p.47. This prominent Malá Strana landmark, below the castle, is Prague's most ornate Baroque church.

6 Charles Bridge > p.60. Prague's famous medieval stone bridge is packed with people and lined with Baroque statues.

7 Museum Kampa > p.52. This art gallery houses a permanent collection of two Czech artists: Kupka, a pioneer in abstract art, and the cubist sculptor Gutfreund.

Dinner > p.57. Try the intimate French restaurant, *Café de Paris*, or for a more grandiose setting, head for the *Savoy* (right).

Day Two in Prague

1 Obecní dům > p.90. Book yourself on the morning tour round this cultural centre, an Art Nouveau jewel built in 1911.

2 Colloredo-Mansfeldský palace > p.64. One of the City Gallery Prague's venues displays contemporary art in a palace setting that combines High Baroque and Rococo.

3 Old Town Square > p.66. Prague's showpiece square, with its parade of Baroque facades, its giant statue of Jan Hus and its interactive astronomical clock.

4 Týn Church > p.68. This giant Gothic church's twin, unequal towers preside over Old Town Square.

Lunch > p.76. *Maitrea* is a smart, cave-like vegetarian restaurant near the Týn Church.

5 Pinkas Synagogue > p.80. Pay your respects to the 77,297 Czech Jews killed in the Holocaust, whose names cover the walls of this sixteenth-century synagogue.

6 Old Jewish Cemetery > p.81. An evocative medieval cemetery in which the crowded gravestones mirror the cramped conditions in the ghetto.

7 Old-New Synagogue > p.79. This thirteenth-century synagogue is the oldest active synagogue in Europe and one of Prague's earliest Gothic buildings.

Dinner > p.75. Try *Lokál* for a homely, traditional Czech meal with great service and fresh Pilsner Urquell beer.

Communist Prague

Despite forty-odd years of Communism, the regime left very few physical traces on the city. However, if you know where to look there are several understated – and one or two ironic – memorials to the period.

1 Kinský Palace > p.67. It was from the balcony of this Baroque palace that Klement Gottwald proclaimed the 1948 Communist takeover.

2 Museum of Communism > p.89. It took an American expat to collect together the city's only collection of Communist memorabilia.

3 Jan Palach memorial > p.86. In 1969, two young men took their own lives in protest against the Soviet invasion of the previous year.

4 Národní > p.98. A simple bronze memorial commemorates the demonstration of November 17, 1989, which sparked the Velvet Revolution.

5 Memorial to the Victims of Communism > p.54. Olbram Zoubek's striking memorial at the floor of Petřín hill pays tribute to the thousands who were imprisoned, executed and went into exile.

6 Míčovna > p.38. Seek out the hammer and sickle added to this Renaissance building in the Royal Gardens by the Communist restorers.

7 Metronome, Letná > p.118. Take in the view from the metronome, which stands in the place where the world's largest Stalin statue once stood.

8 Žižkov Hill > p.115. Once used as a Communist mausoleum, the Žižkov monument still boasts lashings of Socialist Realist decor.

9 Olšany cemeteries > p.114. Pay your respects to the Red Army soldiers who lost their lives liberating the city in May 1945.

Kids' Prague

Most kids will love Prague, with its hilly cobbled streets and trams, especially in summer when the place is alive with street performers and buskers. Prague Castle, with its fairytale ramparts and towers, rarely disappoints either.

1 Funicular > p.55. The funicular at Újezd, which takes you effortlessly to the top of Petřín hill, is part of the public transport system and is a great way to start a day's sightseeing.

2 Petřín > p.54. The Mirror Maze is a guaranteed hit with kids of all ages, and if you need to wear them out even more, get them to walk up the mini-Eiffel Tower for top views.

3 Changing of the Guard > p.33. Prague Castle's armed guards are dressed like toy soldiers, and at noon every day they put on a bit of a show to a melancholic modern melody.

4 Tram #22 > p.138. This tram takes you from Prague Castle, round a hairpin bend and across the river to Karlovo náměstí, a short walk from the PPS terminal.

5 Boat trip > p.138. From April to September, you can take a 45-minute boat ride from PPS terminal near Palackého all the way to Troja, home of the zoo.

6 Prague Zoo > p.124. Prague Zoo has had a lot of money spent on it, and it shows: modern enclosures, sensitive landscaping and everything from elephants to zebras.

BEST OF PRAGUE

Big sights

1 **Old Town Square** The city's showpiece square, lined with exquisite Baroque facades and overlooked by the town hall's famous astronomical clock. > **p.66**

2 Charles Bridge

Decorated with extravagant ecclesiastical statues, this medieval stone bridge is the city's most enduring monument. > **p.60**

3 Josefov

The former Jewish ghetto contains no fewer than six synagogues, a town hall and a remarkable medieval cemetery. > **p.78**

 ## 4 Prague Castle

Towering over the city, the castle is the ultimate picture-postcard image of Prague. > **p.32**

5 Wenceslas Square The modern hub of Prague, this sloping boulevard has been the scene of countless protests over the centuries. > **p.86**

Green Prague

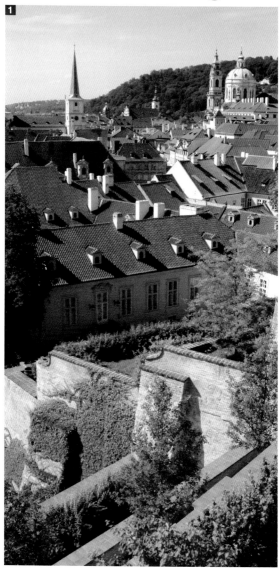

1 Malá Strana terraced gardens Pretty little Baroque gardens laid out on the terraced slopes below the castle. > **p.50**

2 Vyšehrad This old Habsburg military fortress is now a great escape from the busy city. > **p.110**

3 Stromovka Large leafy park laid out between Výstaviště and the chateau of Troja. > **p.123**

4 Royal Gardens Prague Castle's formal gardens are famous for their disciplined crops of tulips. > **p.38**

5 Petřín This wooded hill on Prague's left bank provides a spectacular viewpoint over the city. > **p.54**

Baroque
Prague

1 Loreto church A sumptuous Baroque pilgrimage complex with frescoed cloisters, a Black Madonna, and a stunning array of reliquaries and monstrances. ➤ **p.43**

2 Old Town Square Probably the most impressive parade of Baroque facades and gables in all Prague. > **p.66**

3 Charles Bridge statues It's the (mostly) Baroque statues that make this medieval bridge so unforgettable. > **p.60**

4 Church of sv Mikuláš The city's finest Baroque church, whose dome and tower dominate the skyline of Malá Strana. > **p.47**

5 Strahov Monastery Strahov boasts two monastic libraries with fantastically ornate bookshelves and colourful frescoes. > **p.44**

Cafés

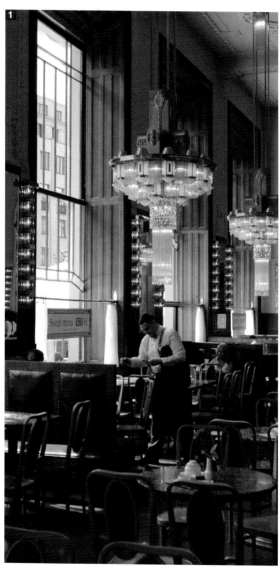

1 Obecní dům Café decor doesn't come better than this Art Nouveau masterpiece. > **p.93**

2 Montmartre Vaulted former haunt of the likes of Kafka, Werfel and Hašek. > **p.74**

3 Grand Café Orient Perfect reconstruction of a first-floor Cubist café from 1911. > **p.74**

4 Café Slavia Immortalized in a poem by Nobel Prize-winner Jaroslav Seifert, this café is haunted by the ghosts of generations of Czech writers. > **p.104**

5 Café Louvre First-floor café that roughly reproduces its illustrious 1902 predecessor. > **p.104**

Museums
and galleries

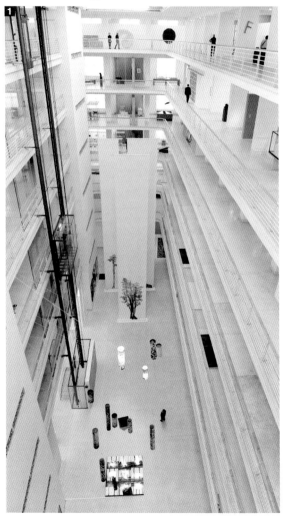

1 Veletržní Palace The city's premier modern art museum is housed in the functionalist Trade Fair Palace. > **p.121**

2 Convent of St Agnes Gothic convent that provides the perfect setting for the national collection of medieval art. > **p.70**

3 UPM A treasure-trove of Czech applied art ranging from Meissen porcelain and Art Nouveau vases to avant-garde photography. > **p.82**

4 Museum Kampa Private collection housed in a converted watermill and stuffed with works by František Kupka, among others. > **p.52**

5 DOX Centre for Contemporary Art Contemporary art creatively displayed in a beautiful space. > **p.121**

Art Nouveau Prague

1 Prague Main Train Station Fight your way through the subterranean modern station and you'll find Josef Fanta's newly renovated 1909 station. **> p.87**

2 Obecní dům Built in 1911 with the help of leading Czech artists, this is the city's finest Art Nouveau edifice. > **p.90**

3 Jan Hus Monument This gargantuan Art Nouveau monument forms the centrepiece of Old Town Square. > **p.68**

4 Mucha's window, St Vitus Cathedral Alfons Mucha's Art Nouveau stained-glass window in St Vitus Cathedral dates from the mid-1920s. > **p.32**

5 Mucha Museum Dedicated to Alfons Mucha, the Czech artist best known for his Parisian posters. > **p.89**

Pubs

1 U medvídků One of the few central pubs that has changed little over the decades. > **p.77**

2 **U kocoura** Old-established Malá Strana pub serving Budvar. > **p.59**

4 **U černého vola** A truly authentic unpretentious pub serving Velkopopovický kozel beer. > **p.45**

3 **Pivovarský dům** Holding its own among the city's newer microbreweries with a good range of pub food. > **p.106**

5 **Letenský zámeček** Great summer terrace overlooking the city and river from Letná. > **p.125**

Nightlife

1 **AghaRTA Jazz Centrum** Prague's best venue for jazz and blues is situated just off Old Town Square. **> p.77**

2 Mecca
This coolly converted factory is one of the most impressive, professional and popular clubs in Prague.
> **p.125**

3 Divadlo Archa
The most adventurous theatre in Prague, with everything from straight theatre to dance and live music.
> **p.95**

4 Roxy City-centre dance club with its finger in all sorts of avant-garde pies. > **p.77**

5 Stavovské divadlo The city's chief opera house has a glittering interior and many Mozart associations.
> **p.77**

PLACES

Prague Castle

Prague's skyline is dominated by the vast hilltop complex of Prague Castle (Pražský hrad), which looks out over the city centre from the west bank of the River Vltava. There's been a royal seat here for over a millennium, and it continues to serve as headquarters of the Czech president, but the castle is also home to several of Prague's chief tourist attractions: the Gothic Cathedral of sv Víta, the late medieval Old Royal Palace, the diminutive and picturesque Golden Lane and numerous museums and galleries. The best thing about the place, though, is that the public are free to roam around the atmospheric courtyards and take in the views from the ramparts from early in the morning until late at night.

CATHEDRAL OF SV VÍTA

Third courtyard ⓦ www.katedralasvatehovita .cz. April–Oct Mon–Sat 9am–5pm, Sun noon–5pm; Nov–March closes 4pm. Entry included with Prague Castle ticket. MAP P.34, POCKET MAP C11

Begun by Emperor Charles IV (1346–78), the **Cathedral** has a long and chequered history and wasn't finally completed until 1929. Once inside, it's difficult not to be impressed by the sheer height of the nave, and struck by the modern fixtures and fittings, especially the **stained-glass windows**, among

them Alfons Mucha's superb *Cyril and Methodius* window, in the third chapel in the north wall, and František Bílek's wooden altar, in the north aisle.

Of the cathedral's numerous side chapels, the grand **Chapel of sv Václav** (better known as Wenceslas, of "Good King" fame), by the south door, is easily the main attraction. The country's patron saint was killed by his pagan brother, Boleslav the Cruel, who later repented, converted, and apparently transferred his brother's remains to this very spot. The chapel's gilded walls are inlaid with over a thousand semiprecious stones, set around ethereal fourteenth-century frescoes of the Passion; meanwhile, the tragedy of Wenceslas unfolds above the cornice in sixteenth-century paintings.

The highlight of the ambulatory is the **Tomb of St John of Nepomuk**, a work of Baroque excess, sculpted in solid silver with free-flying angels holding up the heavy drapery of the baldachin. On the lid of the tomb, back-to-back with John himself, a cherub points to the martyr's severed tongue. Before you leave, check out the Habsburgs' sixteenth-century marble **Imperial Mausoleum**, in the centre of the choir, surrounded by a fine Renaissance grille. Below lies the claustrophobic **Royal Crypt**, resting place of emperors Charles IV and Rudolf II, plus various other Czech kings and queens.

You can also climb the cathedral's **Great Tower** (daily: April–Oct 10am–6pm; Nov–March 10am–5pm; closed in bad weather; 150Kč), from the south aisle. Outside the cathedral, don't forget to clock the **Golden Gate**, above the south door, decorated with a remarkable fourteenth-century mosaic of the Last Judgement.

Visiting the castle

The castle precincts are open daily (April–Oct 5am–midnight; Nov–March 6am–11pm ☏ 224 372 423, ⊛ www.hrad.cz). There are two main types of **multi-entry ticket** available for the sights within the castle (excluding the cathedral). The **long tour** ticket (350Kč) gives you entry to most of the sights within the castle, including the Cathedral of sv Víta, the Old Royal Palace, the Basilica and Convent of sv Jiří, the Prague Castle Picture Gallery and Golden Lane. The **short tour** (250Kč) only covers the Cathedral of sv Víta, the Old Royal Palace, the Basilica of sv Jiří, and Golden Lane. Castle tickets are valid for two days and are available from various ticket offices. Temporary exhibitions, such as those held in the Imperial Stables and Riding School, all have separate admission charges.

Most people **approach the castle** from Malostranská metro station by taking the steep short cut up the Staré zámecké schody, which brings you into the castle from the rear entrance to the east. A better approach is down Valdštejnská, and then up the more stately Zámecké schody, where you can stop and admire the view, or up the cobbled street of Nerudova, before entering the castle via the main gates. From April to October, you might also consider coming up through Malá Strana's wonderful terraced gardens (see p.50), which are connected to the castle gardens. Alternatively, you can take tram #22 from Malostranská metro, which deposits you at the Pražský hrad stop outside the Royal Gardens to the north of the castle.

The hourly **Changing of the Guard** at the main gates is a fairly subdued affair, but every day at noon there's a much more elaborate parade, accompanied by a modern fanfare.

There are a couple of cafés within Prague Castle at which you can grab a coffee and a snack, though you'd be better off outside the castle precincts.

Prague Castle

RESTAURANT
Villa Richter 1

TYCHONOVA

MARIÁNSKÉ HRADBY

Royal Gardens

Zahradní dům

Jízdárna

PRAŠNÝ MOST

Imperial Stables

Prague Castle
Picture Gallery

SECOND
COURTYARD

sv Kříž

FIRST
COURTYARD

ZAHRADA
NA BAŠTĚ

HRADČANSKÉ
NÁMĚSTÍ

T.G. Masaryk

N

Belvedere

Singing
Fountain

Míčovna

Jelení příkop

Brusnice

Powder Tower
(Prašná věž)

VIKÁŘSKÁ

Cathedral
of sv Víta

Zlatá
brána

WC

Obelisk

St George

THIRD COURTYARD

BULL
STAIRCASE

RAJSKÁ
ZAHRADA

ZÁMECKÉ SCHODY

Basilica
of sv Jiří

Convent
of sv Jiří

JIŘSKÉ
NÁMĚSTÍ

JIŘSKÁ

Old Royal
Palace

Hudební
pavilón

South Gardens

Bílá věž

Golden Lane

JIŘSKÁ

Lobkowicz
Palace

Entrance to Malá
Strana palace gardens

Daliborka

Černá
věž

Chotkovy
sady

5 12 18 20 22

CHOTKOVA

STARÉ ZÁMECKÉ SCHODY

22

22

0   metres   100

0   yards   100

34

OLD ROYAL PALACE (STARÝ KRÁLOVSKÝ PALÁC)

Third courtyard. Daily: April–Oct 9am–5pm; Nov–March 9am–4pm. 140Kč. MAP OPPOSITE. POCKET MAP C11

The **Old Royal Palace** is a sandwich of royal apartments, built one on top of the other by successive princes and kings of Bohemia, but left largely unused for the past three hundred years. It was in the **Vladislav Hall**, with its remarkable, sweeping rib-vaulting which forms floral patterns on the ceiling, that the early Bohemian kings were elected, and that every president since 1918 has been sworn into office. From a staircase in the southwest corner, you can climb up to the Bohemian Chancellery, scene of Prague's **second defenestration**, when two Catholic governors, appointed by Ferdinand I, were thrown out of the window by a group of Protestant Bohemian noblemen in 1618. A quick canter down the Riders' Staircase will take you to the Gothic and Romanesque palace chambers containing "**The Story of Prague Castle**", an interesting, if overlong, exhibition on the development of the castle through the centuries.

POWDER TOWER (PRAŠNÁ VĚŽ)

Vikářská. Daily: April–Oct 9am–5pm; Nov–March 9am–4pm. 70Kč. MAP OPPOSITE. POCKET MAP C10

The **Powder Tower** is where Rudolf's team of alchemists were put to work trying to discover the secret of the philosopher's stone. It now houses an exhibition on the history of the Castle Guard.

BASILICA OF SV JIŘÍ

BASILICA OF SV JIŘÍ

Jiřské náměstí. Daily: April–Oct 9am–5pm; Nov–March 9am–4pm. MAP P.34, POCKET MAP C10–11

Don't be fooled by the basilica's russet-red Baroque facade; inside is Prague's most beautiful Romanesque building, meticulously scrubbed clean and restored to re-create something like the honey-coloured stone basilica that replaced the original tenth-century church in 1173. The double staircase to the chancel is a remarkably harmonious late Baroque addition and now provides a perfect stage for chamber music concerts. The choir vault contains a rare early thirteenth-century painting of the New Jerusalem from Revelation, while to the right of the chancel are sixteenth-century frescoes of the burial chapel of sv Ludmila, Bohemia's first Christian martyr and grandmother of St Wenceslas.

Good King Wenceslas

Disappointingly, there's very little substance to the story related in the nineteenth-century English Christmas carol, "Good King Wenceslas looked out". For a start, **Václav (Wenceslas)** was only a duke and never a king (though he did become a saint); he wasn't even that "good", except in comparison with the rest of his family; Prague's St Agnes fountain, by which "yonder peasant dwelt", wasn't built until the thirteenth century; and he was killed a good three months before the Feast of Stephen (Boxing Day) – the traditional day for giving to the poor, hence the narrative of the carol.

Born in 907, Václav inherited his title aged 13. His Christian grandmother, Ludmila, was appointed regent in preference to Drahomíra, his pagan mother, who subsequently had Ludmila murdered in 921. On coming of age in 925, Václav became duke in his own right and took a vow of celibacy, intent on promoting Christianity throughout the dukedom. Even so, the local Christians didn't take to him, and when he began making conciliatory overtures to the neighbouring Germans, they persuaded his pagan younger brother, Boleslav the Cruel, to do away with him. On September 20, 929, Václav was stabbed to death by Boleslav at the entrance to a church just outside Prague.

CONVENT OF SV JIŘÍ (JIŘSKÝ KLÁŠTER)

Jiřské náměstí. MAP P.34, POCKET MAP C10

Bohemia's earliest monastery was founded in 973 by Prince Boleslav II and his sister Mlada, who was its first mother superior. A fire in 1142 resulted in the addition of the main apse and two steeples which are still in place today, while the Early Baroque period saw it given its striking facade. In the eighteenth century invading troops devastated the building, with later architects seeking to revive its original Romanesque style. Until 2012 the convent held an art collection from the National Gallery, but at the time of writing there were no plans to reopen it.

GOLDEN LANE (ZLATÁ ULIČKA)

Daily: April–Oct 9am–5pm; Nov–March 9am–4pm. MAP P.34, POCKET MAP D10

A seemingly blind alley of brightly coloured miniature cottages, **Golden Lane** is by far the most popular sight in the castle, and during the day the whole street is crammed with sightseers. Originally built in the sixteenth century for the 24 members of Rudolf II's castle guard, the lane takes its name from the goldsmiths who followed a century later. By the nineteenth century, the whole street had become a kind of palace slum, attracting artists and craftsmen, its two most famous inhabitants being Nobel Prize-winning poet Jaroslav Seifert, and Franz Kafka, who came here in the evenings to write short stories during the winter of 1916.

LOBKOWICZ PALACE (LOBKOVICKÝ PALÁC)

Jiřská 3 ⓦwww.lobkowicz.cz. Daily 10am–6pm. 275Kč. MAP P.34, POCKET MAP D10

Appropriated in 1939 and again in 1948, and only recently handed back, the Lobkowicz Palace now houses an impressive selection of the Lobkowicz family's prize possessions (with audio-guide accompaniment), including original manuscripts by Mozart and Beethoven, old musical instruments, arms and armour and one or two masterpieces such as a Velázquez portrait, Pieter Brueghel the Elder's sublime *Haymaking* from the artist's famous cycle of seasons, and two views of London by Canaletto.

GOLDEN LANE (ZLATÁ ULIČKA)

SOUTH GARDENS
(JIŽNÍ ZAHRADY)

Daily: April & Oct 10am–6pm; May & Sept 10am–7pm; June & July 10am–9pm; Aug 10am–8pm. Free. MAP P.34, POCKET MAP C11

These gardens, which link up with the terraced gardens of Malá Strana (see p.50), enjoy wonderful vistas over the city. Originally laid out in the sixteenth century, the gardens were remodelled in the 1920s with the addition of an observation terrace and colonnaded pavilion, below which is an earlier eighteenth-century *Hudební pavilón* (music pavilion).

Two sandstone obelisks further east record the arrival of the two Catholic councillors after their 1618 defenestration from the Royal Palace (see p.35).

ROYAL GARDENS
(KRÁLOVSKÁ ZAHRADA)

Daily: April & Oct 10am–6pm; May & Sept 10am–7pm; June & July 10am–9pm; Aug 10am–8pm. Free. MAP P.34, POCKET MAP C10

Founded by Ferdinand I in 1530, the **Royal Gardens** are smartly maintained, with fully functioning fountains and immaculately cropped lawns. It's a popular spot, though more a place for admiring the azaleas and almond trees than lounging around on the grass. Set into the south terrace – from which there are unrivalled views over to the cathedral – is the Renaissance **ball-game court** (Míčovna), occasionally used for concerts and exhibitions. The walls are tattooed with sgraffito and feature a hammer and sickle to the side of one of the sandstone

ROYAL GARDENS

FILIGREE IRONWORK AT THE BELVEDERE

half-columns, thoughtfully added by restorers in the 1950s.

PRAGUE CASTLE PICTURE GALLERY (OBRAZÁRNA PRAŽSKÉHO HRADU)

Second courtyard Ⓦ www.kulturanahrade.cz. Daily: April–Oct 9am–5pm; Nov–March 9am–4pm. 100Kč. MAP P.34, POCKET MAP C11

The remnants of the **imperial collection**, begun by Rudolf II, are housed here. Among the collection's finest paintings is Rubens' richly coloured *Assembly of the Gods at Olympus*, an illusionist triple portrait of Rudolf and his Habsburg predecessors that's typical of the sort of tricksy work that appealed to the emperor. Elsewhere, there's an early, very beautiful *Young Woman at Her Toilet* by Titian, and Tintoretto's *Flagellation of Christ*, a late work in which the artist makes very effective and dramatic use of light.

BELVEDERE (KRALOVSKÝ LETOHRÁDEK)

Mariánské hradby 1. Tues–Sun 10am–6pm. Free. MAP P.34, POCKET MAP D10

Prague's most celebrated Renaissance building is a delicately **arcaded summer-house** topped by an inverted copper ship's hull, begun by Ferdinand I in 1538 for his wife, Anne (though she didn't live long enough to see it completed). The Belvedere's exterior walls are decorated by a series of lovely figural reliefs depicting scenes from mythology, while the interior is used for exhibitions by contemporary artists. In the palace's miniature formal garden is the so-called **Singing Fountain**, named for the musical sound the drops of water make when falling in the metal bowls below.

Restaurant

VILLA RICHTER

Staré zámecké schody 6 ☎ 702 205 108, Ⓦ www.villarichter.cz. Daily 11am–11pm. MAP P.34, POCKET MAP D10

Set amid the castle vineyards, just outside the Black Tower (Černá věž), *Villa Richter* has three separate places one on top of the other: the *Piano Nobile* serves up classy duck, beef and seafood dishes (600–700Kč); below, the *Piano Terra* specializes in Bohemian standards (200–350Kč); and *Panorama Pergola* is the perfect place to sample some Czech wines and soak up the view.

Hradčany

Hradčany – the district immediately outside Prague Castle – is replete with ostentatious Baroque palaces built on an ever-increasing scale. The monumental appearance of these palaces is a direct result of the great fire of 1541, which destroyed the small-scale medieval houses that once stood here and allowed the Habsburg nobility to transform Hradčany into the grand architectural showpiece it still is. Nowadays, despite the steady stream of tourists en route to the castle, it's also one of the most peaceful parts of central Prague, barely disturbed by the civil servants who work in the area's numerous ministries and embassies. The three top sights to head for are the Šternberg Palace, with its collection of Old Masters, the Baroque pilgrimage church of Loreto and the ornate libraries of the Strahov monastery.

Hradčany

CAFÉS
| Malý Buddha | 5 |
| U zavěšenyho kafe | 2 |

RESTAURANTS
| U císařů | 1 |
| U ševce Matouše | 4 |

PUBS
| Klašterní pivovar | 6 |
| U černého vola | 3 |

ACCOMMODATION
Domus Henrici	4
Questenberk	6
Savoy Prague	5
U krále Karla	2
U raka	1
U zlatého koníčka	3

SHOPS
| Antique Musical Instruments | 2 |
| Folk Art | 1 |

0 metres 100
0 yards 100

HRADČANSKÉ NÁMĚSTÍ

MAP OPPOSITE, POCKET MAP B11

Hradčanské náměstí fans out from the castle gates, surrounded by the oversized palaces of the old Catholic nobility. The one spot everyone heads for is the ramparts in the southeastern corner, which allow an unrivalled view over the red rooftops of Malá Strana, and beyond. Few people make use of the square's central green patch, which is heralded by a wonderful giant green wrought-iron lamppost from the 1860s and, behind it, a Baroque plague column. The most noteworthy palaces on the square are the **Schwarzenberg Palace**, at no. 2, with its over-the-top sgraffito decoration, and the sumptuous, vanilla-coloured Rococo **Archbishop's Palace**, opposite.

ŠTERNBERG PALACE

Hradčanské náměstí 15 ⓦ www.ngprague .cz. Tues–Sun 10am–6pm. 150Kč. MAP OPPOSITE, POCKET MAP B11

This elegant early eighteenth-century palace is now an art gallery housing **European Old Masters** from the fourteenth to the eighteenth century. It's a modest collection, though the handful of masterpieces makes a visit here worthwhile, and there's an elegant courtyard café.

The highlights of the first floor include Dieric Bouts' *Lamentation*, a complex composition crowded with figures in medieval garb, two richly coloured Bronzino portraits, and Jan Gossaert's eye-catching *St Luke Drawing the Virgin*, an exercise in architectural geometry and perspective. Before you head upstairs though, don't miss the side room (11) containing Orthodox icons from Venice, the Balkans and Russia.

The second floor boasts a searching portrait of old age by Tintoretto, a wonderfully rugged portrait by Goya and a mesmerizing *Praying Christ* by El Greco. Be sure to admire the Čínský kabinet, a small oval chamber smothered in gaudy Baroque Chinoiserie, and one of the palace's few surviving slices of original decor. Elsewhere, there is a series of canvases by the Brueghel family, a Rembrandt, and Rubens' colossal *Murder of St Thomas* (room 30).

The ground floor contains several superb Cranach canvases, plus one of the most celebrated paintings in the whole collection: the *Feast of the Rosary* by Albrecht Dürer, one of Rudolf II's most prized acquisitions, which he had transported on foot across the Alps to Prague.

SCHWARZENBERG PALACE

Hradčanské náměstí 2 🔘 www.ngprague
.cz. Tues–Sun 10am–6pm. 150Kč. MAP P.40,
POCKET MAP B11

The most outrageous,
over-the-top, sgraffitoed pile on
Hradčanské náměstí now
houses a collection of **Czech
Baroque art**, of only limited
interest to the non-specialist.
Chronologically, you should
begin on the second floor,
where you get a brief glimpse
of the overtly sensual and
erotic Mannerist paintings that
prevailed during the reign of
Rudolf II (1576–1612). The rest
of the gallery is given over to
the art that spearheaded the
Counter-Reformation in the
Czech Lands: paintings by the
likes of Bohemia's Karel Škréta
and Petr Brandl, and the
gesticulating sandstone
sculptures of Matthias
Bernhard Braun and Ferdinand
Maximilian Brokof.

MARTINIC PALACE

Hradčanské náměstí 8 🔘 www
.martinickypalac.cz. Tours must be arranged in
advance on ☎ 777 798 040. 150Kč. MAP P.40,
POCKET MAP B11

Compared to the other palaces
on the square, this is a fairly
modest pile, built in 1620 by
one of the councillors who
survived the second defenestration (see p.35). Its rich sgraffito
decoration, which continues in
the inner courtyard, was only
discovered during restoration
work in the 1970s. On the
facade, you can easily make out
Potiphar's wife making a grab
at a naked and unwilling
Joseph. Guided tours of the
interior – available by
appointment only – show off
some exceptionally well-
preserved Renaissance art as
well as providing a glimpse of
the lifestyle enjoyed by the
palace's original owners. Lovely
Late Renaissance painted
ceilings and frescoes give new
meaning to the term wall art,
and there's a nice display of
typical furnishings from the
Renaissance era.

ČERNÍN PALACE

Loretánské náměstí 5. Closed to the public.
MAP P.40, POCKET MAP A11

Loretánské náměstí is
dominated by the phenomenal
135m-long facade of the
Černín Palace, decorated with
thirty Palladian half-columns
and supported by a row of
diamond-pointed rustication.
Begun in the 1660s, the
building nearly bankrupted
future generations of Černíns,

CERNIN PALACE

who were eventually forced to sell the palace to the Austrian state in 1851, which converted it into military barracks.

Since 1918, the palace has housed the **Ministry of Foreign Affairs**, and during World War II it was, for a while, the Nazi Reichsprotektor's residence. On March 10, 1948, it was the scene of Prague's third – and most widely mourned – defenestration. Only days after the Communist coup, **Jan Masaryk**, the only son of the founder of Czechoslovakia, and the last non-Communist in the cabinet, plunged to his death from the top-floor bathroom window of the palace. Whether it was suicide (he had been suffering from bouts of depression, partly induced by the country's political path) or murder will probably never be satisfactorily resolved, but for most people Masaryk's death cast a dark shadow over the newly established regime.

LORETO

Loretánské náměstí 7 ⓦ www.loreta.cz. Daily: April–Oct 9am–5pm; Nov–March 9.30am–12.15pm & 1–6pm. 150Kč. MAP P.40, POCKET MAP A11

The outer casing of the Loreto church was built in the early part of the eighteenth century – all hot flourishes and Baroque twirls, topped by a bell tower that clanks out the hymn "We Greet Thee a Thousand Times" on its 27 Dutch bells. The focus of the pilgrimage complex is the **Santa Casa** (a mock-up of Mary's home in Nazareth), built in 1626 and smothered in a rich mantle of stucco depicting the building's miraculous transportation from the Holy Land. Pride of place within is given to a limewood statue of the Black Madonna and Child, encased in silver.

LORETO

Behind the Santa Casa, the much larger **Church of the Nativity** has a high cherub count, plenty of Baroque gilding and a lovely organ replete with music-making angels and putti. As in the church, most of the saints honoured in the **cloisters** are women. Without doubt, the weirdest of the lot is St Wilgefortis (Starosta in Czech), whose statue stands in the final chapel of the cloisters. Daughter of the king of Portugal, she was due to marry the king of Sicily, despite having taken a vow of virginity. God intervened and she grew a beard, whereupon the king of Sicily broke off the marriage and her father had her crucified. Wilgefortis thus became the patron saint of unhappily married women, and is depicted bearded on the cross (and easily mistaken for Christ in drag).

You can get some idea of the Loreto's serious financial backing in the church's **treasury**, whose master exhibit is a tasteless Viennese silver monstrance, studded with diamonds taken from the wedding dress of Countess Kolovrat, who made the Loreto sole heir to her fortune.

NOVÝ SVĚT

MAP P.40, POCKET MAP A11

Nestling in a shallow dip in the northwest corner of Hradčany, **Nový Svět** provides a glimpse of life on a totally different scale. Similar in many ways to the Golden Lane in the Hrad – but without the crowds – this picturesque cluster of brightly coloured cottages is all that's left of Hradčany's medieval slums, painted up and sanitized in the eighteenth and nineteenth centuries.

STRAHOV MONASTERY

Strahovské nadvoří 1 Ⓦ www .strahovmonastery.cz. Libraries: daily 9am–noon & 1–5pm; 80Kč. Gallery: daily 9am–noon & 12.30–5pm; 80Kč. MAP P.40, POCKET MAP A12

The Baroque entrance to the Strahov monastery is topped by a statue of St Norbert, who founded the order in 1140 and whose relics were brought here in 1627. The church, which was remodelled in Baroque times, is well worth a peek for its colourful frescoes relating to St Norbert's life, but it's the monastery's two ornate Baroque **libraries** (*knihovny*) that are the real reason for visiting Strahov.

The **Philosophical Hall** has walnut bookcases so tall they almost touch the frescoes on the library's lofty ceiling, while the paintings on the low-ceilinged

Theological Hall are framed by wedding-cake-style stuccowork. Look out, too, for the collection of curios in the glass cabinets outside the library, which features shells, turtles, crabs, lobsters, dried-up sea monsters, butterflies, beetles and plastic fruit. There's even a pair of whales' penises displayed alongside a narwhal horn, harpoons and a model ship.

The monastery's collection of religious art, displayed in the **Strahov Gallery** (*obrazárna*) above the cloisters, contains one or two gems: a portrait of Emperor Rudolf II by his court painter, Hans von Aachen, plus a superb portrait of Rembrandt's elderly mother by Gerrit Dou.

MUSEUM OF MINIATURES

Strahovské nadvoří 11 Ⓦ www .muzeumminiatur.cz. Daily 9am–5pm. 100Kč. MAP P.40, POCKET MAP A12

This small museum displays forty or so works by the Russian **Anatoly Konyenko**, including the smallest book in the world, a thirty-page edition of Chekhov's *Chameleon*. Among the other miracles of miniature manufacture are a flea bearing golden horseshoes, scissors, and a key and lock; the Lord's Prayer written on a human hair; and a caravan of camels passing through the eye of a needle.

STRAHOV MONASTERY

Shops

ANTIQUE MUSIC INSTRUMENTS

Pohořelec 7 & 9. Daily 9am–6pm. MAP P.40.
POCKET MAP A12

More than just lutes and old violins, this place also sells icons, Art Nouveau glass, clocks and model trains and cars.

FOLK ART

Pohořelec 7. Daily 10am–9pm. MAP P.40.
POCKET MAP A12

Specializes in a variety of handcrafted textiles including tablecloths, scarves and purses.

Cafés

MALÝ BUDDHA

Úvoz 46. Tues–Sun noon–10.30pm. MAP P.40.
POCKET MAP A12

Typical Prague teahouse decor, with a Buddhist altar in one corner and good vegetarian Vietnamese snacks on the menu. A very useful smoke-free Hradčany haven.

U ZAVĚŠENÝHO KAFE (THE HANGING CAFÉ)

Úvoz 6. Daily 11am–midnight. MAP P.40. POCKET
MAP B11

A pleasant, smoky crossover café/pub serving cheap beer

and traditional Czech food in a handy spot near the Hrad.

Restaurants

U CÍSAŘŮ (THE EMPEROR)

Loretánská 5 ☎220 518 484. Daily
9am–1am. MAP P.40, POCKET MAP B11

Upmarket medieval place serving up hearty, meaty Czech dishes, as well as trout, butterfish and fondue for 400Kč and upwards.

U ŠEVCE MATOUŠE (THE COBBLER MATOUŠ)

Loretánské náměstí 4 ☎220 514 536.
Daily 11am–4pm & 6–11pm. MAP P.40, POCKET
MAP A11

Fried pork steak served with potato salad (269Kč) is the speciality of this former cobbler's, which is one of the few half-decent places to eat in the castle district.

Pubs

KLAŠTERNÍ PIVOVAR (THE MONASTERY BREWERY)

Strahovské nádvoří 1. Daily 10am–10pm.
MAP P.40, POCKET MAP A12

Tourist-friendly monastic brewery, offering their own light and dark St Norbert beers and Czech pub food.

U ČERNÉHO VOLA (THE BLACK OX)

Loretánské náměstí 1. Daily 10am–10pm.
MAP P.40, POCKET MAP A11

Great traditional Prague pub doing a brisk business serving huge quantities of popular light beer Velkopopovický kozel to thirsty local workers, soaked up with a few classic pub snacks.

Malá Strana

Malá Strana, Prague's picturesque "Little Quarter", sits below the castle and is in many ways the city's most entrancing area. Its many peaceful, often hilly, cobbled backstreets have changed very little since Mozart walked them during his frequent visits to Prague between 1787 and 1791. They conceal a whole host of quiet terraced gardens, as well as the wooded Petřín Hill, which together provide the perfect inner-city escape in the summer months. The Church of sv Mikuláš, by far the finest Baroque church in Prague, and the Museum Kampa, with its unrivalled collection of works by František Kupka, are the two major sights.

MALOSTRANSKÉ NÁMĚSTÍ

MAP P.48–49, POCKET MAP D11

Malostranské náměstí, Malá Strana's arcaded main square, is dominated and divided in two by the Baroque church of sv Mikuláš (see opposite). Trams and cars wind their way across the cobbles below the church, regularly dodged by a procession of people heading up the hill to the castle. On the square's north side at no. 18, distinguished by its two little turrets and rather shocking pistachio and vanilla colour scheme, is the **dům Smiřických**, where, in 1618, the Protestant posse met to decide how to get rid of Emperor Ferdinand's Catholic councillors: whether to attack them with daggers, or, as they eventually attempted, to kill them by chucking them out of the window of the Old Royal Palace (see p.35).

PARLIAMENT

Sněmovna 4 ⓦ www.psp.cz. MAP P.48–49, POCKET MAP D11

The Czech parliament occupies a Neoclassical palace that served as the provincial Diet in the nineteenth century. Later it housed the National Assembly of the First Republic in 1918, the Czech National Council after federalization in 1968, and, since 1993, it has been home to the **Chamber of Deputies** (Poslanecká sněmovna), the (more important) lower house of the Czech parliament. To find out more, visit the **information centre** at Malostranské náměstí 6 (Mon–Fri 9am–4pm).

CHURCH OF SV MIKULÁŠ

Malostranské náměstí ⊚www.stnicholas
.cz. Daily: March–Oct 9am–5pm; Nov–Feb
9am–4pm. 70Kč. MAP P.48–49, POCKET MAP C11–D12

Towering over the whole of
Malá Strana is the Baroque
church of **sv Mikuláš** (St
Nicholas), whose giant green
dome and tower are among the
most characteristic landmarks
on Prague's left bank. Built by
the Jesuits in the early
eighteenth century, it was their
most ambitious project yet in
Bohemia, and the ultimate
symbol of their stranglehold on
the country. Nothing about the
relatively plain west facade
prepares you for the
overwhelming High Baroque
interior. The vast fresco in the
nave portrays some of the more
fanciful miraculous feats of
St Nicholas, while the dome at
the east end of the church is
even more impressive, thanks,
more than anything, to its sheer
height. Leering over you as you
gaze up at the dome are four
terrifyingly oversized and stern
Church Fathers, one of whom
brandishes a gilded thunderbolt,
leaving no doubt as to the
gravity of the Jesuit message. It's
also possible to climb the **tower**
(daily: April–Sept 10am–10pm;
March & Oct 10am–8pm;
Nov–Feb 10am–8pm; 75Kč) for
fine views over Malá Strana and
Charles Bridge.

NERUDOVA

MAP P.48–49, POCKET MAP C11

The busiest of the cobbled
streets leading up to the castle
is **Nerudova**. Historically, this
was the city's main area for
craftsmen, artisans and artists,
though the shops and
restaurants that line Nerudova
now are mostly aimed at
tourists heading for the castle.
Many of the houses that line the
street retain their medieval barn
doors and peculiar pictorial
house signs. One of Nerudova's
fancier buildings, at no. 5, is the
Morzin Palace, now the
Romanian Embassy, its
doorway supported by two
Moors (a pun on the owner's
name). Meanwhile, opposite,
two giant eagles hold up the
portal of the **Thun-Hohenštejn
Palace**, now the Italian
Embassy. Further up the street,
according to legend, Casanova
and Mozart are said to have met
up at a ball given by the
aristocrat owners of no. 33, the
Bretfeld Palace.

47

Malá Strana

Sternberg Palace

Prague Castle Picture Gallery

Cathedral of sv Víta

Prague Castle

Old Royal Palace

sv Jan Nepomucký

Martinic Palace

Archbishop's Palace

St George

South Gardens

KANOVNICKÁ

U LAŽBEN

HRADČANSKÉ NÁM.

sv Kříž

Obelisk

Hudební pavilón

British Embassy

HRADČANY

Schwarzenberg Palace

ZÁMECKÉ SCHODY

THUNOVSK

LORETÁNSKÁ

KE HRADU

ÚVOZ

Bretfeld Palace

NERUDOVA

Morzin Palace

sv Mikulá

N

Instituto Italiano di Cultura

JÁNSKÝ VRŠEK

Liechtenstein Palace

BŘETISLAVOVA

German Embassy

VLAŠSKÁ

VLAŠSKÁ

US Embassy

TRŽIŠTĚ

Vrtbovská zahrada

Panny Marie Vítězné

Mirror Maze

PETŘÍN

Rozhledna

sv Vavřinec

Funicular Railway

Nebozízek

OLYMPISKÁ

K. H. Mácha

CHALOUPECKÉHO

Štefánik Observatory

Hladová zed'

ŠERMÍŘSKÁ

DRTINOVA

ACCOMMODATION

Alchymist Grand Hotel	5
Aria	10
Dientzenhofer	14
Dům U velké boty	4
Little Town Budget Hotel	7
Lokal Inn	6
Lundborg	9
Neruda	2
Nosticova	13
Sax	8
U Karlova mostu	12
U páva	3
U zlaté studně	1
U zlatých nůžek	11

VENUES

Malostranská beseda	1
U malého Glena	2

SHOPS

Ahasver	6
ARTĚL	3
Elima	1
Galerie piva	5
Shakespeare a synové	2
Truhlář marionety	4
Vetešnictví	7

CAFÉS

Bohemia Bagel	10
Cukrkávalimonáda	12
Pekařství v Karmelitské	15
Savoy	24
U knoflíčků	22
U zeleného čaje	5

RESTAURANTS

Bar Bar	19
Café de Paris	16
Gitanes	11
Hergetová cihelná	7
Kampa Park	14
Nebozízek	23
Noi	18
Pálffy palác	1
Rybářský klub	20
U malé velryby	17
U sedmi Švábů	4

PUBS & BARS

Baráčnická rychta	8
Ferdinanda	13
Jo's Bar	9
Malostranská pivnice	6
Mlýnská Kavárna	21
U hrocha	2
U kocoura	3

VALDŠTEJN PALACE

Valdštejnské náměstí 4 ⓌWwww.senat.cz. Tours: April–Oct Sat & Sun 10am–6pm; Nov–March first weekend of the month 10am–4pm. Free. MAP P.48–49, POCKET MAP D11

Built in the 1620s for **Albrecht von Waldstein**, commander of the Imperial Catholic armies of the Thirty Years' War, the Valdštejn Palace was one of the first and largest Baroque palaces in the city. Nowadays, it houses the Czech parliament's upper house, or **Senate** (**Senát**), whose sumptuous Baroque chambers can be visited on a guided tour at weekends.

KAREL ZEMAN MUSEUM

Saská 3 ⓌWwww.muzeumkarlazemana.cz. Daily 10am–7pm. 200Kč. MAP P.48–49, POCKET MAP D12

Czech animator, director and special effects innovator **Karel Zeman** influenced a generation of filmmakers and technicians, from George Lucas and Steven Spielberg to Tim Burton and Terry Gilliam. This museum (opened 2013) covers the director's entire filmography. Exhibits detail the **special effects** techniques used in individual movies, each accompanied by a video showcasing their use. Best of all is the interactive nature of the museum: visitors can record themselves in front of a rear-projected image or film a shoot through a 3D model.

VALDŠTEJNSKÁ ZAHRADA (PALACE GARDENS)

April–May & Oct Mon–Fri 7.30am–6pm, Sat & Sun 10am–6pm; June–Sept till 7pm. Free. MAP P.48–49, POCKET MAP D11

Valdštejn Palace's **formal gardens** are accessible from the palace's main entrance, and also from a doorway in the palace walls along Letenská. The gardens' focus is a gigantic Italianate **sala terrena**, a monumental loggia decorated with frescoes of the Trojan Wars, which stands at the end of an avenue of sculptures. In addition, there are a number of peacocks, a pseudo grotto along the south wall, with quasi-stalactites, and an aviary of eagle owls.

TERRACED PALACE GARDENS

Valdštejnská. Daily: April & Oct 10am–6pm; May–Sept 10am–7pm. 80Kč. MAP P.48–49, POCKET MAP D10

A great way to reach the Castle is via Malá Strana's Baroque **terraced gardens**, on the steep slopes where the royal vineyards used to be. Dotted with urns and statuary, they command superb views over Prague. From Valdštejnská, you enter via the Ledeburská zahrada, gardens which connect higher up with the castle's own South Gardens (see p.38).

THE SALA TERRENA IN THE VALDŠTEJN PALACE'S GARDENS

FRANZ KAFKA MUSEUM

Cihelná 2b ⓦ www.kafkamuseum.cz. Daily 10am–6pm. 200Kč. MAP P.48–49, POCKET MAP E11

This museum offers a fairly sophisticated rundown of the life and works of the Czech–German writer **Franz Kafka** (1883–1924). The first section includes photos of the old ghetto into which Kafka was born, an invoice from his father's shop, with the logo of a jackdaw (*kavka* in Czech), copies of his job applications, requests for sick leave, one of his reports on accident prevention in the workplace, and facsimiles of his pen sketches. Upstairs, audiovisuals and theatrical trickery are used to explore the torment, alienation and claustrophobia Kafka felt throughout his life and expressed in his writings. On a lighter note, don't miss David Černý's **Pissing Figures** (Čůrající postavy) statue in the courtyard outside, which features two men urinating into a pool shaped like the Czech Republic.

MALTÉZSKÉ NÁMĚSTÍ

MAP P.48–49, POCKET MAP D12

Maltézské náměstí is one of a number of delightful little squares between Karmelitská and the river. At the north end is a plague column, topped by a statue of St John the Baptist, but the square takes its name from the Order of the Knights of St John of Jerusalem (now known as the Maltese Knights), who in 1160 founded the nearby church of **Panna Maria pod řetězem** (St Mary below-the-chain), so-called because it was the Knights' job to guard the Judith Bridge (predecessor to Charles Bridge). Only two bulky Gothic towers are still standing and the apse is now thoroughly Baroque, but the nave remains unfinished and open to the elements.

JOHN LENNON WALL

MAP P.48–49, POCKET MAP D12

The pretty little square of **Velkopřevorské náměstí** echoes to the sound of music from the nearby Prague conservatoire, its northern limit marked by the garden wall of the Grand Priory of the Maltese Knights. Here, following John Lennon's death in 1980, Prague's youth established an ad hoc shrine smothered in graffiti tributes to the ex-Beatle. The running battle between police and graffiti artists continued well into the 1990s, with the society of Maltese Knights taking an equally dim view of the mural, but a compromise has now been reached and the wall's scribblings legalized. While you're in the vicinity, be sure to check out the love padlocks which have been secured to the railings of the nearby bridge.

KAMPA

MAP P.48-49, POCKET MAP E12-D13

Heading for **Kampa**, the largest of the Vltava's islands, with its cafés, old mills and serene riverside park, is the perfect way to escape the crowds. The island is separated from the left bank by Prague's "Little Venice", a thin strip of water called **Čertovka** (Devil's Stream), which used to power several millwheels until the last one ceased to function in 1936. For much of its history, the island was the city's main wash-house area, a fact commemorated by the church of **sv Jan Křtitel na Prádle** (St John-the-Baptist at the Cleaners) on Říční. It wasn't until the sixteenth and seventeenth centuries that the Nostitz family, who owned Kampa, began to develop the northern half of the island; the southern half was left untouched, and today is laid out as a public park, with riverside views across to Staré Město. To the north, the oval main square, **Na Kampě**, once a pottery market, is studded with slender acacia trees and cut through by Charles Bridge, to which it is connected by a double flight of steps.

MUSEUM KAMPA

U Sovových mlýnů 2 ⓦ www.museumkampa .cz. Daily 10am–6pm. 240Kč. MAP P.48-49, POCKET MAP D13-E13

Housed in an old riverside watermill, **Museum Kampa** is dedicated to the private art collection of Jan and Meda Mládek. As well as temporary exhibitions, the stylish modern gallery also houses the best of the Mládeks' collection, including a whole series of works by the Czech artist **František Kupka**, seen by many as the father of abstract art. These range from early Expressionist watercolours to transitional pastels like *Fauvist Chair* from 1910, and more abstract works, such as the seminal oil painting, *Cathedral and Study for Fugue in Two Colours*, from around 1912. The gallery also displays a good selection of Cubist and later interwar works by the sculptor **Otto Gutfreund** and a few collages by postwar surrealist Jiří Kolář.

VRTBOVSKÁ ZAHRADA

Karmelitská 25 ⓦ www.vrtbovska.cz. April–Oct daily 10am–6pm. 62Kč. MAP P.48-49, POCKET MAP C12

One of the most elusive of Malá Strana's many Baroque gardens, the **Vrtbovská zahrada** was founded on the site of the former vineyards of the Vrtbov Palace. Laid out on Tuscan-style terraces, dotted with ornamental urns and statues of the gods by Matthias Bernhard Braun, the gardens twist their way up the lower slopes of Petřín Hill to an observation terrace from where there's a spectacular rooftop perspective on the city.

VIEW OF KAMPA FROM CHARLES BRIDGE

CHURCH OF PANNY MARIE VÍTĚZNÉ

Karmelitská 9 🌐 www.pragjesu.info.
Mon–Sat 8.30am–7pm, Sun 8.30am–8pm.
Free. MAP P.48–49, POCKET MAP C12–D12

Surprisingly, given its rather plain exterior, the church of **Panny Marie Vítězné** (Our Lady of Victory) houses a high-kitsch wax effigy of the infant Jesus as a precocious 3-year-old, enthroned in a glass case. Attributed with miraculous powers, this image, known as the **Bambino di Praga** (or Prazské Jezulátko), became an object of international pilgrimage and continues to attract visitors. The *bambino* boasts a vast personal wardrobe of expensive swaddling clothes – approaching a hundred separate outfits at the last count – regularly changed by the Carmelite nuns. Some of these outfits are on display in a small museum, up the spiral staircase in the south aisle, including a selection of his velvet and satin overgarments sent from all over the world.

CZECH MUSIC MUSEUM

Karmelitská 2 🌐 www.nm.cz. Wed–Mon
10am–6pm. 120Kč. MAP P.48–49, POCKET MAP
D12–13

Housed in a former nunnery, the permanent collection of the **Czech Music Museum** (České muzeum hudby) begins with a crazy cut-and-splice medley of musical film footage from the last century. Next up is August Förster's pioneering quarter-tone grand piano from 1924 – you can even listen to Alois Hába's microtonal *Fantazie no. 10,* composed for, and performed on, its three keyboards. After this rather promising start, the museum settles down into a conventional display of old central European instruments, from a precious Baumgartner clavichord and an Amati violin to Neapolitan mandolins and a vast contrabass over 2m in height. Best of all is the fact that you can hear many of the instruments on display being put through their paces at listening posts in each room.

JOSEF SUDEK'S ATELIER

Újezd 30 Ⓦ www.sudek-atelier.cz. Tues–Sun noon–6pm. 10Kč. MAP P.48–49, POCKET MAP D13

Hidden behind the buildings on the east side of the Újezd is a faithful reconstruction of the cute little wooden garden studio, where **Josef Sudek** (1896–1976), the great Czech photographer, lived with his sister from 1927. Sudek moved out in 1958, but he used the place as his darkroom to the end of his life. The twisted tree in the front garden will be familiar to those acquainted with the numerous photo-graphic cycles he based around the studio. The building has only a few of Sudek's personal effects and is now used for temporary exhibitions of other photographers' works.

MEMORIAL TO THE VICTIMS OF COMMUNISM

Újezd/Vítězná. MAP P.48–49, POCKET MAP D14

In 2002, the Czechs finally erected a **Memorial to the Victims of Communism**. The location has no particular resonance with the period, but the memorial itself has an eerie quality, especially when illuminated at night. It consists of a series of statues, self-portraits by sculptor **Olbram Zoubek**, standing on steps leading down from Petřín hill behind, each in varying stages of disintegration. The inscription at the base of the monument reads "205,486 convicted, 248 executed, 4500 died in prison, 327 annihilated at the border, 170,938 emigrated".

PETŘÍN

MAP P.48–49, POCKET MAP A13–C13

The hilly wooded slopes of **Petřín**, distinguished by the Rozhledna, a scaled-down version of the Eiffel Tower, make up the largest green space in the city centre. The tower is just one of several exhibits which survive from the **1891 Prague Exhibition**, whose modest legacy also includes the hill's funicular railway (see opposite). At the top of the hill, it's possible to trace the southernmost perimeter wall of the old city, popularly known as the **Hunger Wall**

ŠTEFÁNIK OBSERVATORY

Ⓦ www.observatory.cz. Tues–Sun, times vary. 65Kč. MAP P.48–49, POCKET MAP B14–C14

At the top of the hill, the Hunger Wall (see opposite) runs southeast from the funicular to Petřín's **Štefánik Observatory**. The small astronomical exhibition inside is hardly worth bothering with, but if it's a clear night, a quick peek through either of the observatory's two powerful telescopes is a treat.

ROZHLEDNA

Ⓦ www.petrinska-rozhledna.cz. Daily: April–Sept 10am–10pm; Oct & March 10am–8pm; Nov–Feb 10am–6pm. 120Kč. MAP P.48–49, POCKET MAP B13

Petřín's most familiar landmark is its lookout tower, or **Rozhledna**, an octagonal interpretation – though a mere fifth of the size – of the Eiffel Tower which shocked Paris in 1889, and a tribute to the city's strong cultural and political links with Paris at the time. The view from the public gallery is terrific in fine weather.

MIRROR MAZE (BLUDIŠTĚ)

Ⓦ www.petrinska-rozhledna.cz. Daily: April–Sept 10am–10pm; Oct & March 10am–8pm; Nov–Feb 10am–6pm. 75Kč. MAP P.48–49, POCKET MAP B13

The **Mirror Maze** is housed in a mini neo-Gothic castle complete with mock drawbridge. As well as a mirror maze, there is an action-packed, life-sized **diorama** of the victory of Prague's students and Jews over the Swedes on Charles Bridge in 1648. The humour of the convex and concave mirrors that lie beyond the diorama is so simple it has both adults and kids giggling away.

(Hladová zeď). Instigated in the 1460s by Emperor Charles IV, it was much lauded at the time as a great public work which provided employment for the burgeoning ranks of the city's destitute (hence its name); in fact, much of the wall's construction was paid for by the expropriation of Jewish property.

FUNICULAR RAILWAY

MAP P.48–49, POCKET MAP B13–C13

The **funicular railway** (*lanová dráha*) for Petřín sets off from a station just off Újezd and runs every 10–15min (daily 9am–11.30pm); public transport tickets and travel passes are valid. At the Nebozízek stop halfway up where the carriages pass each other you can get out and soak up the view at the *Nebozízek* restaurant (see p.58); the top station is closest to the Mirror Maze and Rozhledna.

Shops

AHASVER

Prokopská 3. Tues–Sun 11am–6pm. MAP P.48-49, POCKET MAP D12

A delightful little shop selling antique gowns and jewellery, as well as paintings, porcelain and glass.

ARTĚL

U lužickeho semináře 7. Daily 10am–7pm. MAP P.48-49, POCKET MAP D12

Specializing in handcrafted Bohemian crystal glassware, the shop is a treasure-trove of unique pieces decorated with lovely motifs.

ELIMA

Janský vršek 5. Daily 10.30am–6pm. MAP P.48-49, POCKET MAP C12

This tiny little shop in the backstreets sells beautiful, inexpensive, hand-made Polish pottery from Boleslawiec (Bunzlau).

GALERIE PIVA

Lázeňská 15. Mon–Sat 10am–6pm. MAP P.48-49, POCKET MAP D12

This is a relatively small shop, but it stocks one of the city's most judicious selections of Czech bottled beers.

SHAKESPEARE A SYNOVÉ

U lužického semináře 10. Daily 11am–7pm. MAP P.48-49, POCKET MAP E12

Don't be deceived by the tiny frontage; this is a wonderful, large, rambling well-stocked English-language bookstore in which to while away some time.

TRUHLÁŘ MARIONETY

U lužického semináře 5. Daily 10am–7pm. MAP P.48-49, POCKET MAP D12

Prague is awash with cheap, and frankly quite gawdy, puppets, but the Truhlář family are a cut above the rest. Wooden marionettes off the peg from 1600Kč – bespoke from 12,000Kč.

VETEŠNICTVÍ

Vítězná 16. Mon–Fri 10am–5pm. MAP P.48-49, POCKET MAP D14

Proper Prague bric-a-brac shop jam-packed with everything from old metal signs and Communist memorabilia to glassware and porcelain.

Cafés

BOHEMIA BAGEL

Lázeňská 19 Ⓦ www.bohemiabagel.cz. Daily 7.30am–6pm. MAP P.48-49, POCKET MAP D12

Malá Strana branch of the successful self-service chain (and expat favourite) situated close to Charles Bridge, serving filled bagels, all-day breakfasts, soup and chilli.

CUKRKÁVALIMONÁDA

Lázeňská 7. Daily 9am–7pm. MAP P.48-49, POCKET MAP D12

Very professional and well-run café, serving good brasserie-style dishes, as well as coffee and croissants, with tables overlooking the church of Panna Maria pod řetězem.

CAFÉS ON KAMPA

PEKAŘSTVÍ V KARMELITSKÉ

Karmelitská 20. Mon–Fri 7.30am–6pm, Sat 9.30am–5pm, Sun 10.30am–5pm. MAP P.48–49, POCKET MAP D12

A classic cheap Czech bakery, just off Malostranské náměstí, with a café attached where you can wash down your cakes, pastries and rolls with a coffee.

SAVOY

Vítězná 5. Mon–Fri 8am–10.30pm, Sat & Sun 9am–10.30pm. MAP P.48–49, POCKET MAP D14

An L-shaped Habsburg-era café from 1893 with a superb, neo-Renaissance ceiling; you can just have a coffee or a snack if you want, but it doubles as a very good restaurant, with mains (including lots of seafood) for 380Kč and above.

U KNOFLÍČKŮ (THE LITTLE BUTTON)

Újezd 17. Mon–Fri 9am–6.30pm, Sat & Sun 10am–6.30pm. MAP P.48–49, POCKET MAP D13

This simple *cukrárna* (café selling cakes and sandwiches) offers the full range of ice cream, cakes, coffee and traditional *chlebíčky* (open sandwiches) at countryside prices and is a great place to put together a 100Kč lunch.

U ZELENÉHO ČAJE (THE GREEN TEA)

Nerudova 19. Daily 11am–8pm. MAP P.48–49, POCKET MAP C11

Great little stop-off for a pot of tea or a veggie snack en route to Prague Castle; the only problem is getting a place at one of the four tables.

Restaurants

BAR BAR

Všehrdova 17 ☎ 257 312 246. Daily 11.30am–11.30pm. MAP P.48–49, POCKET MAP D13

Funky cellar restaurant serving healthy Czech and European dishes. The short menu (170–255Kč) includes turkey breast, salmon and *tortellini*.

CAFÉ DE PARIS

Maltezské náměstí 4 ☎ 603 160 718. Daily noon–midnight. MAP P.48–49, POCKET MAP D12

This cosy, family-run restaurant is based on Geneva's famous *Café de Paris*. The short menu's signature dish is beef entrecôte in a creamy sauce composed to a secret recipe (349Kč); there's a tofu version available, too.

GITANES

Tržiště 7 ☎ 257 530 163. Daily noon–midnight. MAP P.48–49, POCKET MAP C12

A surreal interior and well-executed Mediterranean food inspired by Dalmatian and Montenegrin cuisine. Mains 185–625Kč.

HERGETOVÁ CIHELNÁ

Cihelná 2b ☎ 296 826 103. Daily 11.30am–1am. MAP P.48–49, POCKET MAP E11

Slick restaurant serving Tiger prawn starters (395Kč), plus pasta and risotto (325–485Kč), and the odd traditional Czech dish (around 400Kč). The riverside summer terrace overlooks Charles Bridge.

KAMPA PARK

Na Kampě 8b ☎ 296 826 102. Daily 11.30am–1am. MAP P.48–49, POCKET MAP E12

Pink house exquisitely located right by the Vltava on Kampa Island, with a superb fish and seafood menu (mains 600–900Kč), top-class service and tables outside in summer.

NEBOZÍZEK (LITTLE AUGER)

Petřínské sady 411 ☎ 257 315 329. Daily 11am–11pm. MAP P.48–49, POCKET MAP C13

Situated at the halfway stop on the Petřín funicular, the view from *Nebozízek* is superb; there's an outdoor terrace and a traditional Czech menu with game dishes from around 300Kč.

NOI

Újezd 19 ☎ 257 311 411. Daily 11am–1am. MAP P.48–49, POCKET MAP D13

A stylish, atmospheric restaurant dishing out some of the tastiest, spiciest Thai food in Prague (mains 200–300Kč), though it's not great for vegetarians. There's a lovely courtyard patio round the back.

PÁLFFY PALÁC

PÁLFFY PALÁC

Valdštejnská 14 ☎ 257 530 522. Daily 11am–11pm. MAP P.48–49, POCKET MAP D11

The restaurant occupies a grand candle-lit room on the first floor of an old Baroque palace, and features a wonderful outdoor terrace from which you can survey the red rooftops of Malá Strana. The international menu is renowned for its creative dishes (from 390Kč).

RYBÁŘSKÝ KLUB

U Sovových mlýnů 1 ☎ 257 534 200. Daily noon–11pm. MAP P.48–49, POCKET MAP D13

Freshwater fish – carp, catfish, zander and others – baked, grilled or deep fried in breadcrumbs for around 250–400Kč are served up at this unpretentious riverside restaurant situated in the park on Kampa Island.

U MALÉ VELRYBY (THE LITTLE WHALE)

Maltézské náměstí 15 ☎ 257 214 703. Daily 10am–10pm. MAP P.48–49, POCKET MAP D12

Herb-encrusted salmon, succulent steaks and duck (around 300Kč) are all turned out to perfection by the chef at this simple modern restaurant.

U SEDMI ŠVÁBŮ (THE SEVEN SWABIANS)

Janský vršek 14 ☎ 257 531 455. Daily 11am–11pm. MAP P.48–49, POCKET MAP C11

Named after the Grimm brothers' tale, this torch-lit tavern serves up traditional Czech beer and food (180–400Kč) to the occasional accompaniment of medieval shenanigans from fire breathing to sword fighting.

Pubs and bars

BARÁČNICKÁ RYCHTA

Na tržišti 23. Mon–Sat 11am–11pm, Sun 11am–9pm. MAP P.48-49, POCKET MAP C12

Všebaráčnická rychta (as it's also known) is a smoke-free *pivnice* hidden away in the cobbled streets south of Nerudova – at night, approach from Tržiště.

FERDINANDA

Karmelitská 18. Mon–Sat 11am–11pm, Sun 11am–5pm. MAP P.48-49, POCKET MAP C12

The Ferdinand brewery's second pub in Prague has four brews on tap (both their dark and the pale lager 11° are delicious). Good lunch menu (Mon–Fri).

JO'S BAR

Malostranské náměstí 7. Daily 11am–2am. MAP P.48-49, POCKET MAP C12

Jo's is the city's original American backpacker hangout. Though it no longer has quite the same vitality, it remains a good place to meet other travellers. There's a club downstairs.

MALOSTRANSKÁ PIVNICE

Cihelná 3. Daily 11am–midnight, Fri & Sat till 1am. MAP P.48-49, POCKET MAP E11

Be warned: they spot tourists a mile away, but for excellent Pilsner, as well as dark Kozel beers in a quiet courtyard, this *pivnice* is hard to beat.

MLÝNSKÁ KAVÁRNA

Všehrdova 14 (entry from Kampa Park). Daily noon–midnight. MAP P.48-49, POCKET MAP D13

This quiet spot on Kampa Island attracts journalists, politicians and artists, all hanging out around a rough wooden table, at the large bar, or on the terrace.

U HROCHA (THE HIPPOPOTAMUS)

Thunovská 10. Daily noon–11.30pm. MAP P.48-49, POCKET MAP C11

A close-knit bunch of locals fill this small, smoky Czech *pivnice*, which is located close to the British Embassy and serves Pilsner Urquell.

U KOCOURA (THE CAT)

Nerudova 2. Daily noon–10.30pm. MAP P.48-49, POCKET MAP D11

The most famous Czech pub on Nerudova inevitably attracts tourists, but the locals come here too for the Pilsner Urquell and Budvar, plus the obvious Czech stomach-fillers. Be warned: this is a smokers' pub.

Venues

MALOSTRANSKÁ BESEDA

Malostranské náměstí 21 ☎ 257 409 123, ⓦ www.malostranska-beseda.cz. Daily 5pm–midnight. MAP P.48-49, POCKET MAP D11

Malá Strana's refurbished old town hall is once again a great venue for Czech rock bands.

U MALÉHO GLENA (LITTLE GLENN'S)

Karmelitská 23 ⓦ www.malyglen.cz. Live music nightly 7.30pm–1am. MAP P.48-49, POCKET MAP D12

The tiny downstairs stage at *U Malého Glena* hosts an eclectic mix of Latin jazz, bebop and blues. There's a cover charge of 150–200Kč.

U MALÉHO GLENA

Staré Město

Staré Město – literally the "Old Town" – is Prague's most central, vital ingredient. The busiest restaurants and pubs are here, and during the day a gaggle of shoppers and tourists fills its complex and utterly confusing web of narrow byways. Yet despite all the commercial activity, there are still plenty of residential streets, giving the area a lived-in feel that is rarely found in European city centres. At the heart of the district is the Old Town Square (Staroměstské náměstí), Prague's showpiece main square, easily the most magnificent in central Europe, and a great place to get your bearings before heading off into the labyrinthine backstreets. The best approach is from the city's most famous medieval landmark, the statue-encrusted Charles Bridge.

CHARLES BRIDGE (KARLŮV MOST)

MAP P.62–63, POCKET MAP E12

Bristling with statuary and crowded with people, **Charles Bridge** is by far the city's most famous monument. Built in the fourteenth century by Charles IV, the bridge originally featured just a simple crucifix. The first sculpture wasn't added until 1683, when **St John of Nepomuk** appeared. His statue was such a propaganda success

that the Catholic church authorities ordered another 21 to be erected between 1706 and 1714. Individually, only a few of the works are outstanding, but taken collectively, set against the backdrop of the Hrad, the effect is breathtaking.

The bridge is now one of the city's most popular places to hang out, day and night: the crush of sightseers never abates during the day, when the niches created by the

CHARLES BRIDGE AT NIGHT

bridge-piers are occupied by souvenir-hawkers and buskers, but at night things calm down a bit, and the views are, if anything, even more spectacular.

You can climb both of the mighty Gothic **bridge towers** for a bird's-eye view of the masses pouring across. The one on the Malá Strana side (daily: April–Sept 10am–10pm; March & Oct 10am–8pm; Nov–Feb 10am–6pm; 90Kč) features two unequal towers, connected by a castellated arch, which forms the entrance to the bridge. The Staré Město one (same hours and entry fee) is arguably the finer of the two, its eastern facade still encrusted in Gothic cake-like decorations from Peter Parler's workshop.

CHURCH OF SV FRANTIŠEK Z ASSISI (ST FRANCIS OF ASSISI)

Křížovnické náměstí. MAP P.62–63, POCKET MAP F12

Built in the 1680s for the Czech **Order of Knights of the Cross with a Red Star**, the original gatekeepers of the bridge, the interior of this half-brick church is smothered in rich marble and gilded furnishings and dominated by its huge dome, decorated with a vast fresco of *The Last Judgement* and rich marble furnishings.

CHARLES BRIDGE MUSEUM (MUZEUM KARLOVA MOSTU)

Křížovnické náměstí 3 ⓦwww .muzeumkarlovamostu.cz. Daily: May–Sept 10am–8pm; Oct–April 10am–6pm. 170Kč. MAP P.62–63, POCKET MAP F12

Those with an interest in stonemasonry and engineering will enjoy the exhibition; everyone else will probably get more out of the archive film footage.

CHURCH OF SV SALVÁTOR (ST SAVIOUR)

Křížovnické náměstí. MAP P.62–63, POCKET MAP F12

The facade of this church prickles with saintly statues which are lit up attractively at night. Founded in 1593, it marks the beginning of the Jesuits' rise to power and is part of the Klementinum (see p.64). Like many Jesuit churches, its design copies that of the Gesù church in Rome; it's worth a quick look, if only for the frothy stucco plaster-work and delicate ironwork in its triple-naved interior.

Staré Město

CAFÉS
Au Gourmand	8
Bakeshop Praha	6
Beas	9
Country Life	15
Cremeria Milano	18
Grand Café Orient	13
Montmartre	17
Siva	7
Týnska literáni Kavárna	11

RESTAURANTS
Ariana	4
Bellevue	24
Klub Architektů	23
Kogo	16
Lehká hlava	25
Lokál	2
Maitrea	10
Mlýnec	19
Stoleti	27
U provaznice	20
V zátiší	22

PUBS & BARS
Blatnička	21
James Joyce	1
Kozička	5
Prague Beer Museum	3
U medvídků	26
U Rudolfina	12
U zlatého tygra	14

River Vltava

See Josefov map

JOSEFOV

Old Jewish Cemetery
Old-New Synagogue
Ceremonial Hall
Rudolfinum
UPM
Jewish Town Hall
Pinkas Synagogue
Maisel Synagogue
NÁMĚSTÍ JANA PALACHA
STAROMĚSTSKÁ
Památník Jaroslava Ježka
Městská knihovna
New Town Hall
sv František z Assisi
Charles Bridge Museum
Klementinum
Rott Haus
Clam-Gallas Palace
sv Salvátor
Smetana Museum
Colloredo-Mansfeldský Palace
sv Jiljí
Divadlo na zábradlí
Bethlehem Chapel
Náprstek Museum
sv Kříž
Topičův dům
National Theatre (Národní divadlo)
sv Voršila

MOST LEGIÍ — 6 — 9 — 22

N

ACCOMMODATION

Arcadia Old Town	10
Černý slon	4
Cloister Inn	14
Grand Hotel Bohemia	5
Grand Hotel Praha	8
Hostel Prague Týn	3
Josef	2
Lippert Hotel	7
Pachtův Palace	13
Residence Řetězová	11
Ritchie's Hostel	9
Savic	12
Travellers Hostel	1
U medvídků	15
Unitas House	16
U tří bubnů	6

SHOPS

Antik v Dlouhé	1
Art Deco	12
Big Ben Bookshop	3
Botanicus	5
Bric a Brac	4
Celetná Crystal	7
Disko Duck	10
Futurista Universum	15
Gábina Páralová	2
Havelská market	13
Hračky u Zlatého Lva	8
Kubista	9
Manufaktura	11
Monarch	17
Prague Fashion Museum	6
Sparky's	14
Sparta Praha	16

VENUES

AghaRTA Jazz Centrum	4
Chapeau Rouge	2
Estates Theatre	5
National Marionette Theatre	3
Roxy	1

KARLOVA

MAP P.62–63, POCKET MAP F12

As the quickest route between Charles Bridge and the Old Town Square, the narrow street of **Karlova** is packed with people day and night, their attention divided between the tacky souvenir shops and not losing their way. With Europop blaring from several shops, jesters' hats and puppets in abundance, and heaps of dubious jewellery on offer, the whole atmosphere can be a bit oppressive in the height of summer – a more peaceful alternative is to head through the Klementinum's courtyards.

KLEMENTINUM

Karlova 1 ⓦwww.klementinum.com. Daily: April–Oct 10am–5pm; Nov–March 10am–4pm. 220Kč. MAP P.62–63, POCKET MAP F12

As they stroll down Karlova, few people notice the **former Jesuit College** on the north side of the street, which covers an area second in size only to the castle. The Habsburg family summoned the Jesuits to Prague in 1556 to help bolster the Catholic cause in Bohemia, and put them in charge of the entire education system, only to expel them in 1773. The complex now belongs to the university and houses, among other things, the **National Library**. Aside from the ornate **Mirrored Chapel** (Zrcadlová kaple), the Klementinum's most easily accessible attractions are open to the public on a 45-minute **guided tour** (in English). The most spectacular sight is the **Baroque Library**, a long room lined with leather tomes, whose ceiling is decorated with one continuous illusionistic fresco praising secular wisdom, and whose wrought-iron gallery balustrade is held up by wooden barley-sugar columns. Upstairs, at roughly the centre of the Klementinum complex, is the **Astronomical Tower**, from which there's a superb view over central Prague.

COLLOREDO-MANSFELDSKÝ PALACE

Karlova 2 ⓦwww.ghmp.cz. Tues–Sun 10am–6pm. 60Kč. MAP P.62–63, POCKET MAP F12

Colloredo-Mansfeld Palace is one of the city's most astounding examples of **palace architecture**. It was recently revived by City Gallery Prague, and you can take a guided tour to learn about the building's Baroque and Rococo designs, its Gothic, Romanesque and Renaissance influences, and the different owners who have laid claim to it, from counts and princes to the Auersperg family. The gallery doesn't have a permanent exhibition, instead featuring a rolling programme of contemporary art on the fourth floor.

NEW TOWN HALL (NOVÁ RADNICE)

Mariánské náměstí 2. MAP P.62-63, POCKET MAP F12-G12

The most striking features of the rather severe **New Town Hall** are the two gargantuan Art Nouveau statues which stand guard at either corner. The one on the left, looking like Darth Vader, is the "Iron Knight", mascot of the armourers' guild; to the right is the caricatured sixteenth-century Jewish sage and scholar, **Rabbi Löw**. According to legend, Löw was visited by Death on several occasions, but escaped his clutches until he reached the ripe old age of 97, when the Grim Reaper hid in a rose innocently given to him by his (in this case, naked) granddaughter. He is also credited with creating the Golem, a mute Frankenstein's monster type of figure, which periodically ran amok in Prague (see p.83).

MALÉ NÁMĚSTÍ

MAP P.62-63, POCKET MAP G12

A little cobbled square at the eastern end of Karlova, **Malé náměstí** was originally settled by French merchants in the twelfth century and is home to the city's first apothecary, **U zlaté koruny** (The Golden Crown), which was opened by a Florentine in 1353 at no. 13. The former pharmacy boasts beautiful chandeliers and a restored Baroque interior, though it's now a jeweller's. The square's best-known building is the russet-red, neo-Renaissance **Rott Haus**, originally an ironmonger's shop founded by V.J. Rott in 1840. Its facade is smothered in agricultural scenes and motifs inspired by the Czech artist Mikuláš Aleš. At the centre of the square stands a fountain dating from 1560 which retains its beautiful, original wrought-iron canopy; sadly, however, it is no longer functioning.

STARÉ MĚSTO

SMETANA MUSEUM (MUZEUM BEDŘICHA SMETANY)

Novotného lávka 1 ⓦ www.nm.cz. Daily except Tues 10am–5pm. 50Kč. MAP P.62–63, POCKET MAP F12

Housed in a gaily decorated neo-Renaissance building on the riverfront, the **Smetana Museum** celebrates the life and work of the most nationalist of all the great Czech composers. His greatest success as a composer was *The Bartered Bride*, which marked the birth of Czech opera, but he was forced to give up conducting in 1874 with the onset of deafness, and eventually died of syphilis in a mental asylum. Unfortunately, the museum fails to capture much of the spirit of the man, though the views across to the castle are good, and you get to wave a laser baton around in order to listen to his music.

CLAM-GALLAS PALACE (CLAM-GALLASŮV PALÁC)

Mariánské náměstí 2. Open for concerts only. MAP P.62–63, POCKET MAP F12–G12

Despite its size, the **Clam-Gallas Palace** is easy to overlook in a narrow space. It's a typically lavish Baroque affair,

HOUSE FACADE ON STAROMĚSTSKÉ NÁMĚSTÍ

with big and burly *Atlantes* supporting the portals. The Palace's doors are open exclusively for concerts, with regular performances in the Opera Barocca series (ⓦ www .operabarocca.cz).

STAROMĚSTSKÉ NÁMĚSTÍ (OLD TOWN SQUARE)

MAP P.62–63, POCKET MAP G11–G12

Easily the most spectacular square in Prague, **Staroměstské náměstí** is the traditional heart of the city. Most of the brightly coloured houses look solidly eighteenth century, but their Baroque facades hide considerably older buildings. Over the centuries, the square has seen its fair share of demonstrations and battles: the **27 white crosses** set into the paving commemorate the Protestant leaders who were condemned to death on the orders of the Habsburg Emperor in 1621, while the patch of green grass marks the neo-Gothic east wing of the town hall, burned down by the Nazis on the final day of the Prague Uprising in May 1945. Nowadays, the square is lined with café tables in summer and packed with a Christmas market in winter, while tourists pour in all year round to watch the town hall's astronomical clock chime, to sit on the benches in front of the Hus Monument, and to drink in the atmosphere of this historic showpiece.

STARÉ MĚSTO TOWN HALL (STAROMĚSTSKÁ RADNICE)

Staroměstské náměstí 1 MAP P.62–63, POCKET MAP G12

The Staré Město **Town Hall** occupies a whole sequence of houses on Staroměstské náměstí, culminating in an obligatory wedge-tower with a graceful

Gothic oriel. You can check out the historical halls and a few rooms that survived World War II, including two former prison cells (Mon 11am–6pm, Tues–Sun 9am–6pm; 100Kč); it's fun to climb the tower too (open until 8pm; 100Kč, combined ticket with Town Hall tour 160Kč). You can also visit the medieval chapel, which has patches of original wall painting, and wonderful grimacing corbels at the foot of the ribbed vaulting. If you get here just before the clock strikes the hour, you'll be able to watch the Apostles going out on parade.

ASTRONOMICAL CLOCK

Staroměstské náměstí 1. Hourly 9am–9pm. MAP P.62–63, POCKET MAP G12

The most popular sight on Staroměstské náměstí is the town hall's fifteenth-century **Astronomical Clock**, whose hourly mechanical dumbshow regularly attracts a crowd of tourists. Little figures of the Apostles shuffle along, bowing to the audience, while perched on pinnacles below are the four threats to the city as perceived by the medieval mind: Death carrying his hourglass and tolling his bell, the Jew with his

moneybags (since 1945 shorn of his stereotypical beard and referred to as Greed), Vanity admiring his reflection, and a turbaned Turk shaking his head. Beneath the figures, four characters representing Philosophy, Religion, Astronomy and History stand motionless throughout the performance. Finally, a cockerel pops out and flaps its wings to signal that the show's over; the clock then chimes the hour.

KINSKÝ PALACE

Staroměstské náměstí 12 ⓦ www.ngprague .cz. Tues–Sun 10am–6pm. 100Kč. MAP P.62–63, POCKET MAP G11

The largest secular building on Staroměstské náměstí is the Rococo **Kinský Palace**, which is perhaps most notorious as the venue for the fateful speech by the Communist prime minister, **Klement Gottwald**, who walked out onto the grey stone balcony one snowy February morning in 1948, flanked by his Party henchmen, to celebrate the Communist takeover with thousands of supporters packing the square below. The top two floors house a permanent collection of Asian art, plus temporary exhibitions.

JAN HUS MONUMENT

Staroměstské náměstí. MAP P.62–63. POCKET MAP G12

The colossal **Jan Hus Monument** features a turbulent sea of blackened bodies – the oppressed to his right, the defiant to his left – out of which rises the majestic moral authority of Hus himself, a radical religious reformer and martyr from the fifteenth century. On the 500th anniversary of his death, in 1915, the statue was unveiled, but the Austrians refused to hold an official ceremony; in protest, Praguers smothered the monument in flowers. Since then it has been a powerful symbol of Czech nationalism: in March 1939, it was draped in swastikas by the invading Nazis, and in August 1968, it was shrouded in funereal black by Praguers, protesting at the Soviet invasion. The inscription along the base is a quote from the will of pioneering educator John Comenius, one of Hus's seventeenth-century followers, and includes Hus's most famous dictum, *Pravda vitězí*

TÝN CHURCH

(Truth Prevails), which appears on the Czech president's official banner.

CHURCH OF SV MIKULÁŠ

Staroměstské náměstí. Daily 10am–4pm. MAP P.62–63, POCKET MAP G11–12

The destruction of the east wing of the town hall in 1945 rudely exposed the Baroque church of **sv Mikuláš**, built for the Benedictines in 1735. The south front is decidedly luscious, with blackened statuary at every cornice; inside, however, it's a much smaller space, theatrically organized into a series of interlocking curves. It's also rather plainly furnished, partly because it was closed down by Joseph II and turned into a storehouse, and partly because it's now owned by the very "low", modern, Czechoslovak Hussite Church. Instead, your eyes are drawn sharply upwards to the impressive stuccowork, the wrought-iron galleries and the trompe-l'oeil frescoes on the dome.

TÝN CHURCH (TÝNSKÝ CHRÁM)

Celetná 5 🔗 www.tyn.cz. Tues–Sat 10am–1pm & 3–5pm, Sun 10am–noon. Free. MAP P.62–63, POCKET MAP G12

The mighty **Týn church** is by far the most imposing Gothic structure in the Staré Město. Its two irregular towers, bristling with baubles, spires and pinnacles, rise like giant antennae above the arcaded houses which otherwise obscure its facade, and are spectacularly lit up at night. Inside, the church has a lofty, narrow nave punctuated at ground level by black and gold Baroque altarpieces. One or two original Gothic furnishings survive, most notably the pulpit and the fifteenth-century baldachin, housing a winged make sure you admire the distinctive bubbling, stucco portal above the main entrance. The church's massive Gothic proportions – it has the longest nave in Prague after the cathedral – make it a favourite venue for organ recitals and other concerts. After the great fire of 1689, Prague's Baroque artists remodelled the entire interior, adding huge pilasters, a series of colourful frescoes and over twenty side altars. The church has close historical links with the butchers of Prague, who are responsible for the thoroughly decomposed human forearm hanging high up on the west wall, on the right as you enter. It has been here for over four hundred years now, ever since a thief tried to steal the jewels of the Madonna from the high altar. As the thief reached out, the Virgin supposedly grabbed his arm and refused to let go. The next day the congregation of butchers had no option but to lop it off, and it has hung there as a warning ever since.

altar in the north aisle. Behind the pulpit, you'll find another superb winged altar depicting John the Baptist, dating from 1520. The pillar on the right of the chancel steps contains the red marble tomb of **Tycho Brahe**, court astronomer to Rudolf II.

TÝN COURTYARD

MAP P.62–63, POCKET MAP G11

Hidden behind the Týn church is the **Týn courtyard**, also known by its German name, **Ungelt** (meaning "No Money", a pseudonym used to deter marauding invaders), which, as the trading base of German merchants, was one of the first settlements on the Vltava. Later, it was transformed into a palace, only to fall into disrepair under the Communists. The complex has now come full circle and is once again home to various shops, restaurants, hotels and the Dominicans.

CHURCH OF SV JAKUB

Malá Štupartská 6. Daily 9.30am–noon & 2–4pm. Free. MAP P.62–63, POCKET MAP H11

Before entering the church,

ESTATES THEATRE

CONVENT OF ST AGNES
(ANEŽSKÝ KLÁŠTER)

Anežská 12 ⓦwww.ngprague.cz.
Tues–Sun 10am–6pm. 150Kč. MAP P.62–63,
POCKET MAP H10

Prague's oldest surviving
Gothic building, founded in
1233 as a Franciscan convent
for the Order of the Poor
Clares, now provides a fittingly
atmospheric setting for the
city's chief **medieval art collection**. The exhibition is
arranged chronologically,
starting with a remarkable
silver-gilt casket from 1360,
used to house the skull of St
Ludmila. The nine panels from
the Vyšší Brod altarpiece, from
around 1350, are also among
the finest in central Europe.
The real gems of the collection,
however, are the six panels by
Master Theodoric, who painted
over one hundred such
paintings for Charles IV's
castle chapel at Karlštejn. These
larger-than-life, half-length
portraits of saints, church
fathers and so on are full of
intense expression and richly
coloured detail, their
depictions spilling onto the
embossed frames. For a
glimpse of some extraordinary
draughtsmanship, check out

the woodcuts by the likes of
Cranach the Elder and Dürer
– the seven-headed beast in
Dürer's *Apocalypse* cycle is
particularly Harry Potter. As
you exit, you get to see the
inside of the Gothic cloisters
and the bare church that serves
as a resting place for, among
others, Václav I (1205–53) and
St Agnes herself.

ESTATES THEATRE
(STAVOVSKÉ DIVADLO)

Ovocný trh 1. MAP P.62–63, POCKET MAP H12

The lime-green and white
Estates Theatre was built in
the early 1780s for the
entertainment of Prague's
large and powerful German
community and remains one
of the finest Neoclassical
buildings in Prague, reflecting
the enormous self-confidence
of its patrons. The theatre
has a place in Czech history,
too, however, for it was here
that the **Czech national
anthem**, "Kde domov můj?"
("Where is my Home?"),
was first performed. It is
also a place of pilgrimage for
Mozart fans, since it was here
that the premieres of *Don
Giovanni* and *La Clemenza di
Tito* took place – the statue of
a hooded figure by the

entrance commemorates the fact. This is, in fact, one of the few opera houses in Europe that remains intact from Mozart's time (though it underwent major refurbishment during the nineteenth century), and it was used by Miloš Forman to film the concert scenes for his Oscar-winning *Amadeus*.

BETHLEHEM CHAPEL (BETLÉMSKÁ KAPLE)

Betlémské náměstí 4. Daily: April–Oct 10am–6.30pm; Nov–March 10am–5.30pm. 60Kč. MAP P.62–63, POCKET MAP F13

The **Bethlehem Chapel** was founded in 1391 by religious reformists, who, denied the right to build a church, proceeded instead to build the largest chapel in Bohemia, with a total capacity of exactly 3000. Sermons were delivered not in the customary Latin, but in the language of the masses – Czech. From 1402 to 1413, **Jan Hus** preached here, regularly pulling in more than enough commoners to fill the chapel, while the Anabaptist **Thomas Müntzer** also preached here in 1521. Of the original building, only the three outer walls remain, with restored patches of the biblical scenes which

were used to get the message across to the illiterate congregation. The rest is a scrupulous reconstruction, using the original plans and a fair amount of imaginative guesswork.

NÁPRSTEK MUSEUM

Betlémské náměstí 1 ⓦwww.nm.cz. Tues & Thurs–Sun 10am–6pm, Wed 9am–6pm. 100Kč. MAP P.62–63, POCKET MAP H13

Vojta Náprstek, founder of the Náprstek Museum, was inspired by the great Victorian museums of London and turned the family brewery into a museum, initially intending it to concentrate on the virtues of industrial progress. Náprstek's interests gradually shifted towards anthropology, however, and it is his ethnographic collections from the Americas, Australasia and Oceania that are now displayed in the museum. Despite the fact that the museum could clearly do with an injection of cash, it still manages to put on some really excellent temporary ethnographic exhibitions on the ground floor, and also does a useful job of promoting tolerance of different cultures.

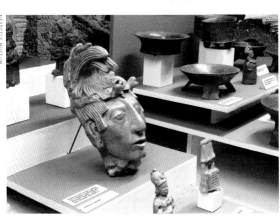

Shops

ANTIK V DLOUHÉ

Dlouhá 37. Mon–Fri 10am–7pm, Sat & Sun noon–6pm. MAP P.62–63, POCKET MAP H11

Great antique shop with many authentic items that will fit in a suitcase, though it does specialize in spectacular light fittings and First Republic chrome tube chairs.

ART DECO

Michalská 21. Mon–Fri 2–7pm, Sat 2–6pm. MAP P.62–63, POCKET MAP G12

A stylish antiques trove made up of clothes, hats, mufflers, teapots, glasses, clocks and art from the first half of the twentieth century.

BIG BEN BOOKSHOP

Malá Štupartská 5. Mon–Fri 9am–8pm, Sat 10am–8pm, Sun 11am–6pm. MAP P.62–63 POCKET MAP H11

Bookstore with probably the widest selection in the city, including cheap paperbacks, kids' books, and lots of magazines and papers.

BOTANICUS

Týn 3. Daily 10am–6.30pm. MAP P.62–63, POCKET MAP H11

Czech take on the UK's Body Shop, with a more folksy ambience. Dried flowers, handmade paper and fancy honey are sold alongside natural soaps and shampoos.

BRIC A BRAC

Týnská 7. Daily 10am–6pm. MAP P.62–63, POCKET MAP G11

Absolutely minute antique store, packed to the rafters with every conceivable trinket. The central location means that prices are quite high, but it's worth visiting for the spectacle alone. The owner also runs a larger place round the corner.

CELETNÁ CRYSTAL

Celetná 15. Daily 10am–7pm. MAP P.62–63, POCKET MAP H12

If you're interested in buying some of the ubiquitous crystal or porcelain that clogs up the city's shop windows, you're sure to get top-quality goods here.

DISKO DUCK

Karlova 12. Daily 12.30–6.30pm. MAP P.62–63, POCKET MAP F12

With some five thousand records in stock, ranging from house, hip hop, r'n'b and techno to electro, jungle and breakbeat, Disko Duck are bound to have something you didn't even know that you needed.

FUTURISTA UNIVERSUM

Betlemské náměstí 5a. Tues–Sun 10am–6.30pm. MAP P.62–63, POCKET MAP F13

Great bookshop offering pricey books on design, architecture and fine art. It also sells groovy posters and arty gifts.

ART DECO

GÁBINA PÁRALOVÁ

Jakubská 14. Mon–Fri noon–7.30pm, Sat 11am–4pm. MAP P.62–63, POCKET MAP H11
Czech fashion designer Gábina Páralová creates casual outfits with surprising details and lively twists, and her shop is a good place to get a fresh look at the Czech fashion scene.

HAVELSKÁ MARKET

Havelská. Mon–Fri 8am–6pm, Sat & Sun 9am–6pm. MAP P.62–63, POCKET MAP G12
Open-air market that stretches the full length of the arcaded street of Havelská, selling fruit, flowers, vegetables, CDs, souvenirs and wooden toys.

HRAČKY U ZLATÉHO LVA

Celetná 32. Daily 10am–7pm. MAP P.62–63. POCKET MAP H12
Multistorey toy shop specializing in wooden playthings, many with a *Krtek* (Little Mole – the most popular Czech cartoon character) theme.

KUBISTA

Ovocný trh 19. Tues–Sun 10am–6.30pm. MAP P.62–63, POCKET MAP H12
Beautiful shop housed in Prague's most impressively preserved Cubist building, selling reproductions of exquisite Cubist ceramics, jewellery and furniture.

MANUFAKTURA

Melantrichova 17. Daily 10am–8pm. MAP P.62–63, POCKET MAP G12
Czech folk-inspired shop with an array of traditional wooden toys, painted Easter eggs, straw decorations, honeycomb candles and kitchen utensils.

MONARCH

Na Perštýně 15. Mon–Sat 3pm–midnight. MAP P.62–63, POCKET MAP G13
Arguably the city's number one wine shop (and wine bar), with

SPARTA PRAHA

stock from all over the world as well as local wine – it sells cheese and dried meats, too.

PRAGUE FASHION MUSEUM

Štupartská 3. Daily 10am–7pm. MAP P.62–62 POCKET MAP H12
Tiny shop showcasing seven decades of fantastic vintage, with stock ranging from clothing and shoes to accessories and jewellery.

SPARKY'S

Havířská 2. Daily 10am–7pm. MAP P.62–63. POCKET MAP H12
Prague's top *dům hraček* (House of Toys) on four floors, which stocks everything from the latest high-tech playthings to traditional wooden toys.

SPARTA PRAHA

Betlémské náměstí 7. Mon–Fri 10am–5pm, Sat 10am–4pm. MAP P.62–63, POCKET MAP G13
Centrally located football-fan shop stocking everything from soccer shirts to ashtrays, mostly for Sparta Praha, but also stocks Slavia Praha, Bohemians and Dukla Praha merchandise.

Cafés

AU GOURMAND

Dlouhá 10. Daily 8am–9pm, Sat & Sun from 8.30am. MAP P.62–63, POCKET MAP G11

Beautifully tiled French boulangerie, patisserie and traiteur selling wickedly delicious pastries; take-away or eat-in. There's another branch in the Palladium shopping centre (see p.92).

BAKESHOP PRAHA

Kozí 1. Daily 7am–9pm. MAP P.62–63, POCKET MAP G11

Three days into a trip to central Europe and already pining for a cupcake or bucket of coffee? Then head to this expat bakery in the very heart of the Old Town.

BEAS

Týnská 19. Mon–Fri 11am–8pm, Sat noon–8pm, Sun noon–6pm. MAP P.62–63, POCKET MAP H11

Bright, modern Indian veggie café through the courtyard off Týnská, offering authentic dosas and thalis served on basic metal trays. Other branches across the capital.

COUNTRY LIFE

Melantrichova 15. Mon–Thurs 10.30am–7.30pm, Fri 10.30am–3.30pm, Sun noon–6pm. MAP P.62–63, POCKET MAP G12

Self-service café behind the health-food shop of the same name: pile up your plate with hot or cold dishes and salad and pay by weight.

CREMERIA MILANO

Husova 12. Mon–Thurs noon–9pm, Fri noon–10pm, Sat 11am–10pm, Sun 11am–9pm. MAP P.62–63, POCKET MAP G12

Multinational *gelateria* that serves up some of the best ice cream in Prague, containing real fruit and nothing it shouldn't.

GRAND CAFÉ ORIENT

Ovocný trh 19. Mon–Fri 9am–10pm, Sat & Sun 10am–10pm. MAP P.62–63, POCKET MAP H12

This superb reconstruction of a famous Cubist café from 1911 dishes up cakes, pancakes and coffee, and there's a lovely narrow balcony for sunny days.

MONTMARTRE

Řetězová 7. Mon–Fri 10am–11pm, Sat & Sun noon–11pm. MAP P.62–63, POCKET MAP F12

Classic, small, barrel-vaulted café, the "Montík" was once a famous First Republic dance and cabaret venue, frequented by the likes of Werfel, Jesenská and Hašek. Nowadays, it's a lot quieter, attracting a good mix of students and locals.

SIVA

Masná 8. Mon–Fri noon–11.30pm, Sat 2–11.30pm, Sun 2–10pm. MAP P.62–63, POCKET MAP H11

A fair stab at a teahouse cellar-den complete with hookah pipes, scatter cushions and passable Arab snacks.

TÝNSKÁ LITERÁRNÍ KAVÁRNA

Týnská 6. Mon–Fri 10am–11pm, Sat & Sun noon–11pm. MAP P.62–63, POCKET MAP G11

City-centre secret with an excellent courtyard perfect for summertime relaxing. The coffee and cakes are decent and there's draught Bernard beer.

Restaurants

ARIANA

Rámová 6 ☎ 222 323 438. Daily 11am–11pm. MAP P.62–63, POCKET MAP H11

Welcoming Afghan restaurant serving up authentic spicy kebabs and veggie dishes (160–250Kč) a stone's throw from the Old Town Square.

BELLEVUE

Smetanovo nábřeží 18 ☎ 222 221 443. Daily noon–3pm & 5.30–11pm. MAP P.62–63, POCKET MAP F13

The view of Charles Bridge and the Hrad is outstanding, the setting is very formal (you must book ahead) and the international cuisine is imaginatively prepared – a two- to five-course dinner will set you back 1190–1490Kč.

KLUB ARCHITEKTŮ

Betlémské náměstí 5A ☎ 224 248 878, ⓦ www.klubarchitektu.com. Daily 11.30am–midnight. MAP P.62–63, POCKET MAP F13

You don't have to be an architect to dine at the candlelit tables of this funky restaurant in the cellars beneath a gallery and design shop. The menu plays it safe with international standards (mains around 300Kč).

KOGO

Havelská 27 ☎ 224 214 543, ⓦ www.kogo.cz. Mon–Thurs 8am–11pm, Fri 8am–1am, Sat 10am–1am, Sun 10am–11pm. MAP P.62–63, POCKET MAP G12

Divided into two intimate spaces by a passageway, and with a small courtyard out back, this place offers decent pasta, pizza and salads for around 275Kč, served by courteous and efficient waiters.

LEHKÁ HLAVA (CLEAR HEAD)

Boršov 2 ☎ 222 220 665, ⓦ www.lehka hlava.cz. Mon–Fri 11.30am–11.30pm,

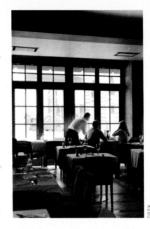

KOGO

Sat & Sun noon–11.30pm. MAP P.62–63, POCKET MAP F13

Exotic cave-like vegetarian restaurant, just off Karoliny Světlé, offering tapas, soups, salads and Mediterranean dishes for 145–195Kč.

LOKÁL

Dlouhá 33 ☎ 222 316 265. Mon–Sat 11am–1am, Sun 11am–10pm. MAP P.62–63, POCKET MAP H11

Vast corridor of a restaurant, decked out in sleek, minimalist decor. Waiters in long white aprons serve up excellent Czech pub food for around 200Kč.

LEHKÁ HLAVA

MAITREA

Týnská ulička 6 ☎ 221 711 631. Mon–Fri 11.30am–11.30pm, Sat & Sun noon–11.30pm. MAP P.62–63, POCKET MAP G11

This larger, more luxurious branch of *Lehká hlava* is a den of stylish Buddhist calm, serving global vegetarian dishes (around 180Kč).

MLÝNEC

Novotného lávka 9 ☎ 277 000 777. Daily noon–3pm & 5.30–11pm. MAP P.62–63, POCKET MAP F12

A pricey place (which has occasionally garnered Michelin stars) with a fabulous riverside terrace overlooking Charles Bridge. Czech staples such as crispy duck and Asian fusion dishes. Set menus from 1390Kč, plus a popular Sunday roast.

STOLETI

Karoliny Světlé 21 ☎ 222 220 008, ⓦwww .stoleti.cz. Daily 11.30am–11.30pm. MAP P.62–63, POCKET MAP F13

Imaginative Czech cuisine named after stars of film and stage served in an unstuffy, simply furnished restaurant. Mains around 250Kč.

U PROVAZNICE

Provaznická 3. Daily 11am–11pm. ☎ 224 232 528, ⓦwww.uprovaznice.cz. MAP P.62–63, POCKET MAP H13

Down a backstreet behind Můstek metro station, this tiled and timbered, tourist-free Czech pub/restaurant plates up no-nonsense Czech favourites at time-warped prices.

V ZÁTIŠÍ (STILL LIFE)

Liliová 1 ☎ 222 221 155. Daily noon–3pm & 5.30–11pm. MAP P.62–63 POCKET MAP F13

Intimate but elegant living-room-sized restaurant serving exquisitely prepared international cuisine, all served in tasty morsels for around 1000Kč for two courses.

Pubs and bars

BLATNIČKA

Michalská 5. Daily 11am–11pm. MAP P.62–63, POCKET MAP G12

Long-established wine shop where you can drink straight from the barrel, take away, or head next door to the popular basement *vinárna* for more wine and inexpensive snacks.

JAMES JOYCE

U Obecního dvora 4 ☎ 224 818 851, ⓦwww .jamesjoyceprague.cz; ⓜ Staroměstská. Mon–Thurs & Sun 11am–12.30am, Fri & Sat 11am–2am. MAP P.62–63, POCKET MAP G10

The best of Prague's Irish pubs, with real Irish staff, an open fire, draught Kilkenny and Guinness and decent Irish-themed food.

KOZIČKA

Kozí 4. Mon–Thurs 4pm–4am, Fri 5pm–4am, Sat 6pm–4am, Sun 7pm–3am. MAP P.62–63, POCKET MAP G11

Busy, designer bare-brick cellar bar with cheap Czech food, tucked away just a short walk from Staroměstské náměstí.

PRAGUE BEER MUSEUM

Dlouhá 46. Daily noon–3am. MAP P.62–63, POCKET MAP H11

For real Czech beer, head to this bar with thirty types on draught, including pilsners, dark lagers, wheat beers, IPAs and more.

KOZIČKA

U MEDVÍDKŮ (THE LITTLE BEARS)

Na Perštýně 7. Mon–Fri 11am–11pm, Sat 11.30am–11pm, Sun 11.30am–10pm. MAP P.62–63, POCKET MAP G13

A Prague beer hall going back to the thirteenth century and still much the same as it always was (make sure you turn right when you enter, and avoid the bar to the left). The Budvar flows freely, and the food is reliably Bohemian.

U RUDOLFINA

Křížovnická 10. Daily 11am–11pm. MAP P.62–63, POCKET MAP F11

A proper Czech *pivnice* serving beautifully kept Pilsner Urquell and typical pub grub, very close to Charles Bridge.

U ZLATÉHO TYGRA (THE GOLDEN TIGER)

Husova 17. Daily 3–11pm. MAP P.62–63, POCKET MAP F12

Small central *pivnice*, always busy with locals and tourists trying to get a seat; the late writer and Bohemian, Bohumil Hrabal, was a semi-permanent resident.

Clubs and venues

AGHARTA JAZZ CENTRUM

Železná 16 ☎222 211 275, 🌐www.agharta .cz. Daily 7pm–1am. MAP P.62–63, POCKET MAP G12

A great central jazz club, with a mix of Czechs and foreigners, a consistently good programme of gigs and a round-the-year festival that brings in some top acts. Cover charge 250Kč.

CHAPEAU ROUGE

Jakubská 2 🌐www.chapeaurouge.cz; Mon–Thurs noon–4am, Fri noon–6am, Sat 4pm–6am, Sun 4pm–3am. MAP P.62–63, POCKET MAP H11

Centrally located, multifloor,

ROXY

good-time club, with a blood-red bar on the ground floor (free entry) and two dancefloors above featuring either DJs or live bands. Cover charge 50–100Kč.

ESTATES THEATRE (STAVOVSKÉ DIVADLO)

Ovocný trh 1 ☎224 901 448, 🌐www .narodni-divadlo.cz. MAP P.62–63, POCKET MAP H12

Prague's oldest opera house has a glorious nineteenth-century interior and puts on a mixture of theatre, ballet and opera (with English subtitles).

NATIONAL MARIONETTE THEATRE

Žatecká 1 ☎224 819 322, 🌐www .mozart.cz. MAP P.62–63, POCKET MAP F11

It could be corny but this is actually good fun – Mozart's operas performed by giant marionettes. They do an early kids' show of *The Magic Flute*.

ROXY

Dlouhá 33 ☎224 826 296, 🌐www.roxy.cz. Daily from 7pm. MAP P.62–63, POCKET MAP H11

Roxy is a great little venue: a laidback, rambling old theatre with a programme ranging from arty films and exhibitions to top live acts and DJ nights. Cover varies: free–250Kč.

Josefov

The old Jewish ghetto district of Josefov remains one of the most remarkable sights in Prague and an essential slice of the city's cultural heritage. Although the warren-like street plan of the old ghetto was demolished in the 1890s to make way for streets of luxurious five-storey mansions, six synagogues, the Jewish town hall and the medieval cemetery still survive. They were preserved under the Nazis as a record of communities they had destroyed. To this end, Jewish artefacts from Czechoslovakia and beyond were gathered here, and today make up one of the most comprehensive collections of Judaica in Europe.

PAMÁTNÍK JAROSLAVA JEŽKA

Kaprova 10 Ⓦ www.nm.cz. Tues 1–6pm. 10Kč.
MAP BELOW, POCKET MAP G11

If you happen to be in the Josefov area on a Tuesday afternoon, it's worth taking the opportunity to visit the Památník Jaroslava Ježka, which occupies one room of the first-floor flat of the avant-garde composer Jaroslav Ježek (1906–42), at Kaprova 10. It's a great way to escape the crowds, hear some of Ježek's music, and

Josefov

SHOPS
Chez Parisienne 3
Judaica 2
La Bretagne 1

VENUES
Rudolfinum 1

PUBS & BARS
Barock 4
Tretter's 8
V kolkovně 5

RESTAURANTS
Dinitz 1
James Dean 9
King Solomon 11
La Veranda 2
Les Moules 3
Pizzeria Rugantino 10
U golema 12

CAFÉS
Nostress 7
Paneria 13
Rudolfinum 6

OLD-NEW SYNAGOGUE (STARONOVÁ SYNAGOGA)

Červená 2. Daily except Sat: April–Oct 9am–6pm; Nov–March 9am–5pm. 200Kč. MAP OPPOSITE, POCKET MAP G11

The **Old-New Synagogue** (**Staronová synagoga** or Altneuschul) got its strange name from the fact that when it was built it was indeed very new, though eventually it became the oldest synagogue in Josefov. Begun in the second half of the thirteenth century, and featuring a wonderful set of steep, sawtooth brick gables, it is, in fact, the oldest functioning synagogue in Europe, one of the earliest Gothic buildings in Prague and still the religious centre for Prague's Orthodox Jews. To get to the **main hall**, you must pass through one of the two low vestibules from which women watch the proceedings through narrow slits. Above the entrance is an elaborate tympanum covered in the twisting branches of a vine tree, its twelve bunches of grapes representing the tribes of Israel. The simple, plain interior is mostly taken up with the elaborate wrought-iron cage enclosing the bimah in the centre. The tattered red standard on display was originally a gift to the community from Emperor Ferdinand II for helping fend off the Swedes in 1648.

admire the Modrý pokoj (Blue Room), with its functionalist furniture and grand piano, in which he did his composing.

NÁMĚSTÍ JANA PALACHA

MAP OPPOSITE, POCKET MAP F11

On the Josefov riverfront is náměstí Jana Palacha, previously known as Red Army Square and embellished with a flowerbed in the shape of a red star (now replaced by an anonymous circular vent), in memory of the Soviet dead who were temporarily buried here in May 1945. The building on the east side of the square is the Faculty of Philosophy, where Jan Palach (see p.86) was a student (his bust adorns a corner of the building).

Visiting Josefov's sights

All the major sights of Josefov – the Old-New Synagogue, Old Jewish Cemetery, the Ceremonial Hall, the Maisel, Pinkas, Klausen and Spanish synagogues – are part of the **Jewish Museum** (ⓦwww .jewishmuseum.cz) and covered by an **all-in-one ticket**, available from any of the quarter's numerous **ticket offices** (main office at U staré školy 1). This costs 480Kč including the Old-New Synagogue, or 300Kč without. **Opening hours** vary but are basically daily except Saturday and Jewish holidays April–October 9am–6pm and November–March 9am–4.30pm.

JEWISH TOWN HALL (ŽIDOVSKÁ RADNICE)

Maiselova 18. Not open to the public. MAP P.78, POCKET MAP G11

The **Jewish Town Hall** is one of the few such buildings in central Europe to survive the Holocaust. Founded and funded by Mordecai Maisel, minister of finance to Rudolf II, in the sixteenth century, it was later rebuilt as the creamy-pink Baroque house you now see. The belfry has a clock on each of its four sides, plus a Hebrew one, stuck on the north gable, which, like the Hebrew script, goes "backwards".

MAISEL SYNAGOGUE (MAISELOVA SYNAGOGA)

Maiselova 10. MAP P.78, POCKET MAP G11

Like the town hall, the neo-Gothic **Maisel Synagogue** was founded and paid for entirely by Mordecai Maisel. Set back from the neighbouring houses south down Maiselova, the synagogue was, in its day, one of the most ornate in Josefov. Nowadays, its bare whitewashed neo-Gothic interior houses an exhibition on the history of the Czech–Jewish community up until the 1781 Edict of Tolerance. Along with glass cabinets filled with gold and silverwork, Hanukkah candlesticks, Torah scrolls and other religious artefacts, there's also an example of the antiquated ruffs that had to be worn by all unmarried males from the age of twelve, and a copy of Ferdinand I's decree enforcing the wearing of a circular yellow badge.

PINKAS SYNAGOGUE (PINKASOV SYNAGOGA)

Široká 3. MAP P.78, POCKET MAP F11

Built in the 1530s for the powerful Horovitz family, the **Pinkas Synagogue** has undergone countless restorations over the centuries. In 1958, the synagogue was transformed into a chilling memorial to the 77,297 Czech Jews killed during the Holocaust. The memorial was closed shortly after the 1967 Six Day War – due to damp, according to the Communists – and remained so, allegedly due to problems with the masonry, until it was finally, painstakingly restored in the 1990s. All that remains of the synagogue's original decor today is the ornate bimah surrounded by a beautiful wrought-iron grille, supported by barley-sugar columns.

Of all the sights of the Jewish quarter, the **Holocaust memorial** is perhaps the most moving, with every bit of wall space taken up with the carved stone list of victims, stating simply their name, date of birth and date of death or transportation to the camps. It is the longest epitaph in the world, yet it represents a mere fraction of those who died in the Nazi concentration camps. Upstairs in a room beside the women's gallery, there's also a harrowing exhibition of drawings by children from the Jewish ghetto in Terezín, most of whom were killed in the camps.

OLD JEWISH CEMETERY (STARÝ ŽIDOVSKÝ HŘBITOV)

Široká 3. MAP P.78, POCKET MAP F11

At the heart of Josefov is the **Old Jewish Cemetery**, which you enter from the Pinkas Synagogue and leave by the Klausen Synagogue. Established in the fifteenth century, it was in use until 1787, by which time there were an estimated 100,000 people buried here, one on top of the other, six palms apart, and as many as twelve layers deep. The enormous number of visitors has meant that the graves themselves have been roped off to protect them, but if you get there before the crowds – a difficult task for much of the year – the cemetery can be a poignant reminder of the ghetto, its inhabitants subjected to inhuman overcrowding even in death. The rest of Prague recedes beyond the tall ash trees and cramped perimeter walls, the haphazard headstones and Hebrew inscriptions casting a powerful spell. On many graves you'll see pebbles, some holding down *kvitlech* or small messages of supplication.

CEREMONIAL HALL (OBŘADNÍ SÍN)

U starého hřbitova. MAP P.78, POCKET MAP F11

Immediately on your left as you leave the cemetery is the **Ceremonial Hall**, a lugubrious neo-Renaissance house built in 1906 as a ceremonial hall by the Jewish Burial Society. Appropriately enough, it's now devoted to an exhibition on Jewish traditions of burial and death, though it would probably be more useful if you could visit it before heading into the cemetery, rather than after.

KLAUSEN SYNAGOGUE (KLAUSOVA SYNAGOGA)

U starého hřbitova 1. MAP P.78, POCKET MAP F11

A late seventeenth-century building, the **Klausen Synagogue** was founded in the 1690s by Mordecai Maisel on the site of several small buildings (Klausen), in what was then a notorious red-light district of Josefov. The ornate Baroque interior contains a rich display of religious objects from embroidered *kippah* to Kiddush cups, and explains the very basics of Jewish religious practice, and the chief festivals or High Holidays.

OLD JEWISH CEMETERY

PAŘÍŽSKÁ

UPM (MUSEUM OF DECORATIVE ARTS)

17 listopadu 2 Ⓜ www.upm.cz. Tues 10am–7pm, Wed–Sun 10am–6pm (closed for refurbishment at the time of writing). 120Kč.
MAP P.78, POCKET MAP F11

From its foundation in 1885 through to the end of the First Republic, the **Uměleckoprůmyslové muzeum** or **UPM** received the best that the Czech modern movement had to offer – from Art Nouveau to the avant-garde – and its collection is consequently unrivalled. The building itself is richly decorated in mosaics, stained glass and sculptures, and its ground-floor temporary exhibitions are consistently excellent. The permanent collection begins on the first floor with the Votive Hall, which is ornately decorated with trompe-l'oeil wall hangings, lunette paintings and a bewhiskered bust of Emperor Franz-Josef I. Next door is the "Story of a Fibre", which is dominated by a double-decker costume display: richly embroidered religious vestments above and fashionable attire from the eighteenth century to modern catwalk concoctions below.

"Born in Fire" is home to the museum's impressive glass, ceramic and pottery displays, from eighteenth-century Meissen figures to Art Nouveau Lötz vases. The "Print and Image" room is devoted mainly to Czech photography, and includes numerous prints from the art form's interwar heyday, including several works by František Drtikol, Jaromír Funkes and Josef Sudek. Finally, in the Treasury, there's a kind of modern-day Kunstkammer or cabinet of curiosities:

PAŘÍŽSKÁ

MAP P.78, POCKET MAP E10–G11

Running through the heart of the old ghetto is **Pařížská**, the ultimate bourgeois avenue, lined with buildings covered in a riot of late nineteenth-century sculpturing, spikes and turrets. At odds with the rest of Josefov, its ground-floor premises are home to designer label clothes and accessory shops, jewellery stores and swanky cafés, restaurants and bars.

RUDOLFINUM

Alšovo nábřeží 12. Tues–Sun 10am–6pm.
MAP P.78, POCKET MAP F11

The **Rudolfinum**, or House of Artists (Dům umělců), is one of the proud civic buildings of the nineteenth-century Czech national revival. Built to house an art gallery, museum and concert hall for the Czech-speaking community, it became the seat of the new Czecho-slovak parliament from 1919 until 1941 when it was closed down by the Nazis. Since 1946, the building has returned to its original artistic purpose and it's now one of the capital's main concert venues (home to the Czech Philharmonic) and exhibition spaces.

everything from ivory objets d'art and seventeenth-century Italian *pietre dure* (hardstone mosaics) to miniature silver furniture and a goblet made from rhino horn.

SPANISH SYNAGOGUE (ŠPANĚLSKÁ SYNAGOGA)

Vězeňská 1. MAP P.78, POCKET MAP G11

Begun in 1868, the **Spanish Synagogue** is by far the most ornate synagogue in Josefov, its stunning, gilded Moorish interior deliberately imitating the Alhambra (hence its name). Every available surface is smothered with a profusion of floral motifs and geometric patterns, in vibrant reds, greens and blues, which are repeated in the synagogue's huge stained-glass windows. The synagogue now houses an interesting exhibition on the history of Prague's Jews from the time of the 1781 Edict of Tolerance to the Holocaust. Lovely, slender, painted cast-iron columns hold up the women's gallery, where the displays include a fascinating set of photos depicting the old ghetto at the time of its demolition. There's a section on Prague's German–Jewish writers, including Kafka, and information on the Holocaust. In the upper-floor prayer hall, there's an exhibition of silver religious artefacts, a fraction of the six thousand pieces collected here, initially for Prague's Jewish Museum, founded in 1906, and later under the Nazis.

The Golem

Legends concerning the animation of unformed matter (which is what the Hebrew word **golem** means), using the mystical texts of the Kabbala, were around long before Frankenstein started playing around with corpses. The most famous golem was the giant servant made from the mud of the Vltava by **Rabbi Löw**, the sixteenth-century chief rabbi of Prague. It was brought to life when the rabbi placed a *shem*, a tablet with a magic Hebrew inscription, in its mouth.

There are numerous versions of the tale, though none earlier than the nineteenth century. In some, the golem is a figure of fun, flooding the rabbi's kitchen rather in the manner of Disney's *Sorcerer's Apprentice*; others portray him as the guardian of the ghetto, helping Rabbi Löw in his struggle with the anti-Semites at the court of Rudolf II. In almost all versions, however, the golem finally runs amok and Löw has to remove the *shem* once and for all, and hide the creature away in the attic of the Old-New Synagogue, where it has supposedly resided ever since – ready to come out again if needed.

Shops

CHEZ PARISIENNE

Pařížská 8. Mon–Fri 10am–7pm, Sat 10am–6pm, Sun 11am–6pm. MAP P.78, POCKET MAP G11

Prague's sexiest lingerie store takes its name from the city's most fashion-conscious street Pařížská.

JUDAICA

Široká 7. Daily except Sat 10am–6pm. MAP P.78, POCKET MAP F11

Probably the best stocked of all the places selling Jewish books to tourists, with books and prints, secondhand and new.

LA BRETAGNE

Široká 22. Mon–Sat 9.30am–7.30pm. MAP P.78, POCKET MAP G11

There's a wide array of fresh fish and seafood at this centrally located fishmonger's, plus takeaway sushi.

Cafés

NOSTRESS

Dušní 10. Daily 10am–midnight. MAP P.78, POCKET MAP G11

Grandly touted as a French-Asian fusion restaurant, this smart-ish café is more of a handy place to enjoy a coffee amid the designer furniture in between synagogues.

PANERIA

Kaprova 3. Mon–Sat 7.30am–8pm, Sun 7.30am–7pm. MAP P.78, POCKET MAP F11

Central branch of a large chain of Czech bakeries specializing in sandwiches, toasted panini and pastries.

RUDOLFINUM

Alšovo nábřeží 12. Tues–Sun 10am–7.30pm. MAP P.78, POCKET MAP F11

Gloriously grand nineteenth-century café on the first floor of the old parliament building – you don't have to visit the gallery to go to the café.

Restaurants

DINITZ

Bílková 12 ☎ 222 244 000. Mon–Thurs & Sun 11.30am–10pm, Fri 11.30am–4.30pm. MAP P.78, POCKET MAP G11

Kosher restaurant with Middle Eastern snacks, sandwiches, pasta, salads (200–350Kč) and mains (350–550Kč).

JAMES DEAN

V Kolkovně 1 ☎ 606 979 797, Ⓦ www .jamesdean.cz. Mon–Fri 8am–4am, Sat & Sun 9am–4am. MAP P.78, POCKET MAP G11

This retro American diner has an authentic-looking interior, huge condiment bottles, ceiling fans, a twangy soundtrack and waitresses dressed for the part. Portions of burgers and fries are Cadillac size. Mains 250–450Kč.

KING SOLOMON

Široká 8 ☎ 224 818 752. Mon–Thurs & Sun noon–11.30pm. Fri dinner & Sat lunch are reservation only. MAP P.78, POCKET MAP F11

Sophisticated kosher restaurant which serves big helpings of international dishes and

U GOLEMA

Maiselova 8 ☎ 222 328 165, ⊕ www
.restaurantugolema.cz. Daily 10am–11.30pm.
MAP P.78, POCKET MAP G11

Golem himself greets diners at
this pleasant restaurant in the
heart of Josefov's sightseeing
zone. Filling meat-themed menu
consisting mainly of Czech food
with a few French influences
(mains around 300Kč).

Pubs and bars

BAROCK

Pařížská 24. Daily 10am–1am. MAP P.78,
POCKET MAP G11

This is the café-bar of choice
for the upwardly mobile locals
who shop on fashionable
Pařížská – the tagline is the
cringe-inducing "delicious meal
and beautiful women".

TRETTER'S

V kolkovně 3. Daily 7pm–3am. MAP P.78, POCKET
MAP G11

Wonderfully smart and
sophisticated (but not
exclusive) American cocktail
bar, with very professional staff
and a celebrity ambience.

V KOLKOVNĚ

V kolkovně 8. Daily 11am–midnight. MAP P.78,
POCKET MAP G11

Justifiably popular with passing
tourists, this Pilsner Urquell
pub has plush new decor,
excellent pub food and
unpasteurized Pilsner on tap.

Venues

RUDOLFINUM

Alšovo nábřeží 12 ☎ 227 059 227, ⊕ www
.ceskafilharmonie.cz. MAP P.78, POCKET MAP F11

A stunning neo-Renaissance
concert hall from the late
nineteenth century that's home
of the Czech Philharmonic.

traditional Jewish specialities: a
three-course set menu (with a
beer) will set you back 550Kč.

LA VERANDA

Elišky Krásnohorské 10 ☎ 224 814 733.
Mon–Sat noon–midnight. MAP P.78, POCKET MAP
G11

Family-run restaurant focused
on locally sourced ingredients
and fresh cooking, with
wonderful staff who really add
to the experience – take their
recommendations when
ordering. Mains (285–485Kč)
range from tagliatelle with
rabbit ragout to brook trout.

LES MOULES

Pařížská 19 ☎ 222 315 022. Daily
11.30am–midnight. MAP P.78, POCKET MAP G11

One of a chain of wood-
panelled Belgian brasseries
which flies in fresh mussels
(666Kč for a bottomless
portion), serving them with
French fries and Belgian beers.

PIZZERIA RUGANTINO

Dušní 4 ☎ 222 318 172. Mon–Sat 11am–11pm,
Sun noon–11pm. MAP P.78, POCKET MAP G11

This pizzeria, just off Dlouhá, is
the real deal: an oak-fired oven,
thin bases and lots of different
toppings (around 200Kč).

Wenceslas Square and northern Nové Město

Nové Město – Prague's "New Town" – is the city's main commercial and business district, housing most of its big hotels, cinemas, nightclubs, fast-food outlets and department stores. Architecturally, it comes over as big, bourgeois and predominantly *fin de siècle*, yet the large market squares and wide streets were actually laid out way back in the fourteenth century by Emperor Charles IV. The obvious starting point in Nové Město is Wenceslas Square (Václavské náměstí), the long, sloping boulevard with its distinctive, interwar shopping malls, which is where Czechs traditionally gather when they have something to protest about and is today at the hub of the modern city.

WENCESLAS SQUARE (VÁCLAVSKÉ NÁMĚSTÍ)

MAP P.86, POCKET MAP H13– J13

The natural pivot around which modern Prague revolves, **Wenceslas Square** is more of a wide, gently sloping boulevard than a square as such. It's scarcely a conventional – or even convenient – space in which to hold mass demonstrations, yet for the past 150 years or more it has been the focus of political protest in Prague. In August

1968 it was the scene of some of the most violent confrontations between the Soviet invaders and the local Czechs. More happily, in late November 1989, more than 250,000 people crammed into the square night after night, often enduring sub-zero temperatures, to demand free elections.

Despite the square's history and its medieval origins, it is now a thoroughly modern, glitzy, slightly seedy boulevard, lined with self-important six- or seven-storey buildings representing every artistic trend of the last hundred years, from neo-Renaissance to Socialist Realism. At the top of the square, in front of the grandiose National Museum, stands the **Wenceslas Monument**, a worthy and heroic, but pretty unexciting, equestrian statue of the country's patron saint. Below the statue, a simple memorial commemorating the victims of Communism is adorned with flowers and photos of Jan Palach and Jan

Zajíc, both of whom martyred themselves here in 1969 in protest at the Soviet invasion.

LUCERNA

MAP P.88, POCKET MAP H14

Wenceslas Square has an impressive array of old shopping arcades, or *pasáže*, as they're known in Czech, mostly dating from the interwar period. The king of the lot is the lavishly decorated *fin de siècle* **Lucerna** *pasáž*, stretching all the way from Štěpánská to Vodičkova. Designed in the early part of the twentieth century in Moorish style by, among others, Václav Havel's own grandfather, it boasts an ornate cinema, café and vast concert hall. Suspended from the ceiling in the centre of the arcade is David Černý's parody of the square's equestrian Wenceslas Monument, with the saint astride an upside-down charger.

NATIONAL MUSEUM (NÁRODNÍ MUZEUM)

Václavské náměstí 68 www.nm.cz. Closed at the time of writing. MAP P.88, POCKET MAP J14

Built in 1890, the broad, brooding hulk of the **National Museum** dominates the view up Wenceslas Square like a giant golden eagle with outstretched wings. When it finally reopens after drawn-out and much delayed renovation work, museum chiefs promise a focus on interactive natural history displays. Be sure to admire the ornate marble entrance hall and splendid monumental staircase leading to the glass-domed Pantheon, with its 48 busts and statues of bewhiskered Czech men (plus a couple of token women and Slovaks). Those with a museum itch might head next door to the **New Building** (Vinohradská 1; daily 10am–6pm; 160Kč), with exhibitions ranging from Czech archeology to scientific and cultural milestones.

PRAGUE MAIN TRAIN STATION (PRAHA HLAVNÍ NÁDRAŽÍ)

MAP P.88, POCKET MAP K13

Prague's main train station is one of the final architectural glories of the dying Habsburg Empire, designed by **Josef Fanta** and officially opened in 1909 as the Franz-Josefs Bahnhof. Arriving by metro, or buying tickets in the over-polished subterranean modern section, it's easy to miss the station's recently renovated Art Nouveau parts. Upstairs, the original entrance – now blighted by a motorway outside – still exudes imperial confidence, with its wrought-iron canopy and naked figurines clinging to the sides of the towers.

Wenceslas Square & northern Nové Město

CAFÉS

Cukrárna v galerii myšák	14
Dobrá čajovna	11
Góvinda	1
Imperial	4
Kavárna Muzeum	19
Lucerna	16
Obecní dům	8
Pekářství Moravec	3
Tramvaj	13
Vesmírna	20

VENUES

Divadlo Archa	1
Kino Lucerna	4
Lucerna Music Bar	3
Obecní dům – Smetanova Síň	2
Prague State Opera	5

RESTAURANTS

Čestr	18
Como	15
Francouzská restaurace	7
Hybernia	9
Modrý zub	10
Monarchie	17
Pizza Nuova	5
Plzeňská restaurace	6
U sádlů	2

SHOPS

Antikvariát v dlážděné	3
Baťa	5
Bontonland	4
Cellarius	7
Kotva	1
Palladium	2
U Sherlocka Holmese	6

ACCOMMODATION

Alcron	7
Harmony	1
Hostel Rosemary	5
Imperial	2
Palace	6
Paříž	4
Salvator	3

PUB

Bredovský dvůr	12

JUBILEE SYNAGOGUE

Jeruzalémská. April–Oct daily except Sat 11am–5pm. 80Kč. MAP OPPOSITE, POCKET MAP J12

Named in honour of the sixtieth year of the Emperor Franz-Josef I's reign in 1908, the **Jubilee Synagogue** was built in an incredibly colourful Moorish style similar to that of the Spanish Synagogue in Josefov, but with a touch of Art Nouveau. The Hebrew quote from Malachi on the facade strikes a note of liberal optimism: "Do we not have one father? Were we not created by the same God?"

JINDŘÍŠSKÁ VĚŽ

MAP OPPOSITE, POCKET MAP J12

This freestanding fifteenth-century tower is the belfry of the nearby church of **sv Jindřich** (St Henry), whose digitally controlled, high-pitched bells ring out every fifteen minutes, and play an entire medley every four hours. In contrast to every other surviving tower in Prague, the **Jindříšská věž** has been imaginatively and expensively restored and now contains a café, restaurant, shop, exhibition space and, on the top floor, a small **museum** (daily 10am–6pm; 90Kč) on Prague's hundred-plus towers, with a good view across the city's rooftops.

MUCHA MUSEUM

Panská 7 ⓦ www.mucha.cz. Daily 10am–6pm. 180Kč. MAP OPPOSITE, POCKET MAP H12–13

Alfons Mucha (1860–1939) made his name in *fin de siècle* Paris, where he shot to fame after designing Art Nouveau posters for the actress Sarah Bernhardt. "Le Style Mucha" became all the rage, but the artist himself came to despise this "commercial" period of his work, and, in 1910, Mucha moved back to his homeland and threw himself into the national cause, designing patriotic stamps, banknotes and posters for the new republic. The whole of Mucha's career is covered in the permanent exhibition, and an excellent video (in English) covers the decade of his life he devoted to the cycle of nationalist paintings known as the Slav Epic.

MUSEUM OF COMMUNISM (MUZEUM KOMUNISMU)

Na příkopě 10 ⓦ www.muzeumkomunismu.cz. Daily 9am–9pm. 190Kč. MAP OPPOSITE, POCKET MAP H12

Above a casino, on the first floor of the Savarin Palace, the **Museum of Communism** gives a brief rundown of twentieth-century Czech history, accompanied by a superb collection of Communist statues, film footage and propaganda posters. The politics are a bit simplistic – the popular postwar support for the Party is underplayed – but it's worth tracking down for the memorabilia alone.

JUBILEE SYNAGOGUE

POWDER TOWER (PRAŠNÁ BRÁNA)

Daily: April–Sept 10am–10pm; March & Oct 10am–8pm; Nov–Feb 10am–6pm. 90Kč. MAP P.88, POCKET MAP H12

One of the eight medieval gate-towers that once guarded Staré Město, the Powder Tower was begun by King Vladislav Jagiello in 1475, shortly after he'd moved into the royal court, which was situated next door at the time. Work stopped when he retreated to the Hrad to avoid the wrath of his subjects; later on, it was used to store gunpowder – hence the name and the reason for the damage incurred in 1757, when it blew up. Most people, though, ignore the small historical exhibition inside, and climb straight up for the modest view from the top.

OBECNÍ DŮM (MUNICIPAL HOUSE)

Náměstí Republiky 5 ⦿ www.obecni-dum.cz. Daily 10am–7pm. MAP P.88, POCKET MAP H11–12

Attached to the Powder Tower, and built on the ruins of the old royal court, the **Obecní dům** is by far the most exciting Art Nouveau building in Prague, one of the few places that still manages to conjure up the atmosphere of Prague's turn-of-the-twentieth-century café society. Conceived as a cultural centre for the Czech community, it's probably the finest architectural achievement of the Czech national revival, extravagantly decorated inside and out by the leading Czech artists of the day. From the lifts to the cloakrooms, just about all the furnishings remain as they were when the building was completed in 1911.

The simplest way of soaking up the interior – peppered with mosaics and pendulous brass chandeliers – is to have a coffee in the cavernous **café** (see p.93). For a more detailed inspection of the building's spectacular interior, you can sign up for one of the regular **guided tours** at the ground-floor information centre (daily 10am–7pm; 290Kč).

BANKA LEGIÍ

Na poříčí 24. Mon–Fri 9am–5pm. Free. MAP P.68, POCKET MAP J11

The **Banka legií** (now a branch of the ČSOB) is one of Prague's most unusual pieces of corporate architecture. A Rondo-Cubist building from the early 1920s, it boasts a striking white marble frieze by Otto Gutfreund, depicting the epic march across Siberia under-taken by the Czechoslovak

OBECNÍ DŮM

Legion and their embroilment in the Russian Revolution, set into the bold smoky-red moulding of the facade. You're free to wander into the main ground-floor banking hall, which retains its curved glass roof and distinctive red-and-white marble patterning.

PRAGUE MUSEUM

Na poříčí 52 ⓌWⓌ www.muzeumprahy.cz. Tues–Sun 9am–6pm. 120Kč. MAP P.88, POCKET MAP K11/E5

Next to Prague's main coach station, a purpose-built neo-Renaissance mansion houses the **Prague Museum**. Inside, there's an ad hoc collection of the city's art, a number of antique bicycles, and usually an intriguing temporary exhibition on some aspect of the city. The museum's prize possession, though, is Antonín Langweil's paper model of Prague which he completed in the 1830s. It's a fascinating insight into early nineteenth-century Prague – predominantly Baroque, with the cathedral incomplete and the Jewish quarter "unsanitized" – and, consequently, has served as one of the most useful records for the city's restorers. The most surprising thing, of course, is that so little has changed.

POSTAL MUSEUM (POŠTOVNÍ MUZEUM)

Nové mlýny 2 Ⓦ www.postovnimuzeum.cz. Tues–Sun 9am–noon & 1–5pm. 50Kč. MAP P.88, POCKET MAP J10

Housed in the **Vávrův dům**, an old mill near one of Prague's many water towers, the **Postal Museum** contains a series of jolly nineteenth-century wall paintings of Romantic Austrian landscapes, and a collection of drawings on postman themes. The real philately is on the ground floor – a vast international collection of stamps arranged in vertical pull-out drawers. The Czechoslovak issues are historically and artistically interesting, as well as of appeal to collectors. Stamps became a useful tool in the propaganda wars of the last century; even such short-lived ventures as the Hungarian-backed Slovak Soviet Republic of 1918–19 and the Slovak National Uprising of autumn 1944 managed to print special issues. Under the First Republic, the country's leading artists, notably Alfons Mucha and Max Švabinský, were commissioned to design stamps, some of which are exceptionally beautiful.

Shops

ANTIKVARIÁT V DLÁŽDĚNÉ

Dlážděná 7. Mon–Fri 9am–6pm, Sat 9am–1pm. MAP P.88, POCKET MAP J12

One of the city centre's longest-established and best second-hand bookstores, but it's the prints and original artwork, some by well-known artists, that many come here for.

BAŤA

Václavské náměstí 6. Mon–Fri 9am–9pm, Sat 9am–8pm, Sun 10am–8pm. MAP P.88, POCKET MAP H13

Functionalist flagship store of Baťa shoe empire, with five floors of fancy footwear located on Wenceslas Square.

BONTONLAND

Václavské náměstí 1. Mon–Fri 9am–8pm, Sat 10am–8pm, Sun 10am–7pm. MAP P.88, POCKET MAP H13

In the *pasáž* at the bottom of Wenceslas Square, Prague's biggest record store sells rock, folk, jazz and classical CDs, DVDs and video games.

CELLARIUS

Štěpánská 61. Mon–Sat 9.30am–9pm, Sun 3–8pm. MAP P.88, POCKET MAP H13

Very well-stocked shop in the Lucerna *pasáž*, where you can taste and take away Czech wines.

KOTVA

Revoluční 1. Mon–Fri 9am–8pm, Sat 10am–7pm, Sun 10am–6pm. MAP P.88, POCKET MAP H11

A seminal piece of dreadful brown 1970s architecture, Kotva is a good old-fashioned Czech department store, with prices to suit all pockets.

PALLADIUM

Náměstí Republiky 1. Thurs–Sat 9am–10pm, Sun–Wed 9am–9pm. MAP P.88, POCKET MAP J11

The apotheosis of Czech consumerism, this is the country's largest shopping mall, occupying spruced-up former barracks opposite Obecní dům.

U SHERLOCKA HOLMESE

Vodičkova 38. Mon–Fri 6am–11pm, Sat & Sun 9am–11pm. MAP P.88, POCKET MAP H14

This calls itself a "cigar and pipe shop", but you'll find other sorts of smoking paraphernalia here too, plus plenty of bottles of spirits, including absinthe.

Cafés

CUKRÁRNA V GALERII MYŠÁK

Vodičkova 31. Mon–Fri 9am–8pm, Sat & Sun 10am–8pm. MAP P.88, POCKET MAP H13

Stylish version of the traditional *cukrárna*, with chandeliers, high-stacked gateaux and tasty ice cream. The interior evokes interwar Czechoslovakia.

DOBRÁ ČAJOVNA

Václavské náměstí 14. Mon–Fri 10am–9.30pm, Sat & Sun 2–9.30pm. MAP P.88, POCKET MAP H13

Mellow, rarefied teahouse, with an astonishing variety of teas (and a few Middle Eastern snacks) served by sandal-wearing waiters.

IMPERIAL

GÓVINDA

Soukenická 27. Mon–Fri 11am–6pm, Sat noon–4pm. MAP P.88, POCKET MAP J10

Daytime Hare Krishna (Haré Kršna in Czech) restaurant with very basic decor, serving organic Indian veggie dishes for just 95Kč.

IMPERIAL

Na poříčí 15. Daily 7am–11pm. MAP P.88, POCKET MAP J11

Built in 1914, and featuring the most incredible ceramic friezes on its walls, pillars and ceilings, the *Imperial* is a must for fans of outrageously sumptuous Art Nouveau decor. You can just come for a coffee, but they also serve breakfast, light lunches and main dishes for 300Kč or so.

KAVÁRNA MUZEUM

Vinohradská 1. Mon–Fri 9am–7pm, Sat & Sun 10am–7pm. MAP P.88, POCKET MAP J14

Large bright café with a mix of high tables and cosy nooks. Located in the National Museum's New Building, people come for the excellent lunch menu and high-quality coffee. Service is cafeteria-style.

LUCERNA

Vodičkova 36. Daily 10am–midnight. MAP P.88, POCKET MAP H14

Wonderfully lugubrious *fin de siècle* café-bar on the first floor, en route to the cinema of the same name, with lots of faux marble and windows overlooking the Lucerna *pasáž.*

OBECNÍ DŮM

Náměstí Republiky 5. Daily 7.30am–11pm. MAP P.88, POCKET MAP H11–12

The vast *kavárna*, with its famous fountain, is a glittering Art Nouveau period piece. Food is nice enough, but most folk come here for a coffee and something from the cake trolley.

PEKÁŘSTVÍ MORAVEC

Biskupský dvůr 1. Mon–Fri 6.30am–6.30pm, Sat 8am–1.30pm. MAP P.88, POCKET MAP K10

Rural Bohemia-style bakery, on a quiet square next to the completely unvisited Church of sv Petra, selling traditional cakes, pastries, ice cream and coffees. A great spot for an authentically early Czech breakfast.

TRAMVAJ

Václavské náměstí. Mon–Sat 9am–midnight, Sun 10am–midnight. MAP P.88, POCKET MAP H13

Two vintage no. 11 trams stranded in the middle of Wenceslas Square (where they used to run) have been converted into a café – a convenient spot for coffee, and easy to locate.

VESMÍRNA

Ve Smečkách 5. Mon–Fri noon–9pm. MAP P.88, POCKET MAP H14

Used as a training café for people with learning difficulties, *Vesmírna* is a popular, cosy spot serving crepes, sandwiches and Czech cakes.

TRAMVAJ

Restaurants

ČESTR

Legerova 75 ☎ 222 727 851, ⓦ cestr.ambi.cz.
Mon–Fri 11.30am–11pm, Sat noon–11pm, Sun
noon–10pm. MAP P.88, POCKET MAP J14

Modern, bright and airy (think
tiles and pine), this place
specializes in matured steaks,
plus fish for the less carnivo-
rous. Mains 200–628Kč.

COMO

Václavské náměstí 45 ☎ 222 247 240. Mon–
Fri 6.30pm–1am, Sat & Sun 7pm–1am. MAP
P.88, POCKET MAP J13

High-quality eating on
Wenceslas Square is a rarity, so
this place is to be cherished.
There are sushi sets and Czech
food, but the Mediterranean
dishes shine. Mains 265–595Kč.

FRANCOUZSKÁ RESTAURACE

Obecní dům, Náměstí Republiky 5 ☎ 222 002
770, ⓦ www.francouzskarestaurace.cz. Daily
noon–11pm. MAP P.88, POCKET MAP H11

The Art Nouveau decor in this
cavernous Obecní dům
restaurant is stunning and the
French-style main dishes
(400–700Kč) are superb.

HYBERNIA

Hybernská 7 ☎ 224 226 004, ⓦ www
.hybernia.cz. Mon–Fri 8am–midnight, Sat &
Sun 11am–midnight. MAP P.88, POCKET MAP J12

Busy restaurant, with a nice
outdoor terrace out the back;
specializes in *špízy* (needles),
aka kebabs, but also serves
good-value Czech food and
pasta dishes (135–295Kč).

MODRÝ ZUB (BLUE TOOTH)

Jindřišská 5 ☎ 222 212 622. Mon–Fri
11am–11pm, Sat noon–11pm, Sun
noon–10pm. MAP P.88, POCKET MAP H13

Good-value Thai rice and
noodle dishes (175–275Kč) in a
place that has a modern
wine-bar feel to it – popular
with Wenceslas Square shoppers.

MONARCHIE

Štěpánská 61 ☎ 296 236 513, ⓦ www
.restaurace-monarchie.cz. Mon–Fri 11am–11pm,
Sat 5–11pm. MAP P.88, POCKET MAP H14

Imperial coats of arms line the
walls at this interesting new
restaurant in the entrance to the
Lucerna *pasáž*. The Austro-
Bohemian menu includes
Wiener schnitzel, suckling pig,
and Pilsen goulash. Mains
260–350Kč.

PIZZA NUOVA

Revoluční 1 ☎ 221 803 308, ⓦ pízzanuova
.ambi.cz. Daily 11.30am–11.30pm. MAP P.88,
POCKET MAP H11

Big and stylish, this upstairs
pizza and pasta place (each
around 200Kč) affords great
views of the trams wending their
way through Náměstí Republiky.

ČESTR

PLZEŇSKÁ RESTAURACE

Obecní dům, Náměstí Republiky 5
☎ 222 002 770, ⓦ www.plzenskarestaurace
.cz. Daily 11.30am–11pm. MAP P.86, POCKET MAP
H11

Decent Czech beer hall-restaurant in the cellar of the Obecní dům, cheaper than the *Francouzská restaurace* upstairs (main dishes 250–400Kč), but not quite the same aesthetic experience.

U SÁDLŮ

Klimentská 2 ☎ 222 252 411, ⓦ www
.usadlu.cz. Mon–Thurs 11am–midnight, Fri &
Sat 11am–1am, Sun noon–midnight. MAP P.88,
POCKET MAP H11

Deliberately over-the-top themed medieval banqueting hall offering a hearty Czech menu, with classics such as roast pork knuckle and goulash (115–520Kč) helped down with lashings of frothing Budvar.

Pubs and bars

BREDOVSKÝ DVŮR

Politických vězňů 12. Mon–Sat 11am–
midnight, Sun 11am–11pm. MAP P.88, POCKET MAP
J13

Popular, brick-vaulted city pub, off Wenceslas Square, serving standard pub food washed down with Pilsner Urquell or Velkopopovický kozel.

Venues

DIVADLO ARCHA

Na poříčí 26 ☎ 221 716 333, ⓦ www
.divadloarcha.cz. MAP P.88, POCKET MAP J11

The city's most innovative venue, with two versatile spaces, an art gallery and café. The programme of music, dance and theatre emphasizes new, experimental work, often with English subtitles or translation.

OBECNÍ DŮM

KINO LUCERNA

Vodičkova 36 ☎ 224 216 972, ⓦ www
.kinolucerna.cz. MAP P.88, POCKET MAP H14

Grandiose 1909 cinema that eschews dubbed films and shows English-subtitled Czech films.

LUCERNA MUSIC BAR

Vodičkova 36 ☎ 224 217 108, ⓦ www
.musicbar.cz. Daily 9.30am until end of event.
MAP P.88, POCKET MAP H14

Scruffy basement bar that attracts some great musicians, local and touring, during the week, before descending into pop disco at the weekend. Cover 100Kč and upwards.

OBECNÍ DŮM – SMETANOVA SÍŇ

Náměstí Republiky 5 ☎ 222 002 101, ⓦ www
.obecni-dum.cz. MAP P.88, POCKET MAP H12

Fantastically ornate Art Nouveau concert hall which usually kicks off the Prague Spring festival and is home to the Prague Symphony Orchestra.

PRAGUE STATE OPERA (STÁTNÍ OPERA PRAHA)

Wilsonova 4 ☎ 224 227 266, ⓦ www
.narodni-divadlo.cz. MAP P.88, POCKET MAP J14

Sumptuous nineteenth-century opera house, originally built by the German-speaking community. It now holds opera, ballet and drama performances.

Národní and southern Nové Město

Off the conventional tourist trail, and boasting only a few minor sights, the network of cobbled streets immediately to the south of Národní is nevertheless great to explore, as it harbours a whole range of interesting cafés, pubs, restaurants and shops that have steadily colonized the area over the past two decades. Southern Nové Město also boasts the city's finest stretch of waterfront, with a couple of leafy islands overlooked by magnificent *fin de siècle* mansions that continue almost without interruption south to Vyšehrad.

JUNGMANNOVO NÁMĚSTÍ

MAP OPPOSITE, POCKET MAP G13

Jungmannovo náměstí is named for **Josef Jungmann** (1772–1847), a prolific writer, translator and leading light of the Czech national revival, whose pensive, seated statue surveys the small, rather ill-proportioned square. The square itself boasts a couple of Czech architectural curiosities, starting with a unique **Cubist streetlamp** (and seat) from 1912, in the far eastern corner. The most imposing building is the chunky, vigorously sculptured **Palác Adria**, designed in Rondo-Cubist style in the early 1920s, with sculptural extras by Otto Gutfreund and a central *Seafaring* group by Jan Štursa. The building's *pasáž* (arcade) still retains its wonderful original portal featuring sculptures depicting the twelve signs of the zodiac. The theatre in the basement was the underground nerve centre of the 1989 Velvet Revolution, where the Civic Forum thrashed out tactics in the dressing rooms and gave daily press conferences in the auditorium against the stage set for Dürenmatt's *Minotaurus*.

THE WATERFRONT IN SOUTHERN NOVÉ MĚSTO

Národní & southern Nové Město

RESTAURANTS		PUBS & BARS		CAFÉS	
Cicala	20	Branický sklípek	9	Café 35 –	
Dynamo	11	Novoměstský pivovar	14	Institut Français	17
Miss Saigon	19	Pivovarský dům	22	Café Louvre	3
Pizzeria Kmotra	12	U Flekù	15	Café Slavia	2
Posezení u Čiriny	18	U havrana	21	Friends Coffee House	4
Renommé	10	U kruhu	6	Marathon	16
Střelecký ostrov	7	U Pinkasù	1	St Tropez	5
Žofín Garden	13	Výloha Bar	24	Svatováclavská	
				Cukrárna	23
				Velryba	8

SHOPS		CLUBS & VENUES		
Bazar	9	Divadlo Minor	7	
Globe	8	Evald	1	
Gold Pralines	6	Laterna magika	5	ACCOMMODATION
Jan Pazdera	5	MAT Studio	8	Hostel Emma
Krakatit	3	National Theatre	4	Hotel 16 –
MPM	7	Nebe	6	U sv Kateřiny
My národní	4	Reduta	2	Hotel Jungmann
Pylones	1	Rock Café	3	Icon Hotel
Quasimodo				Mánes
Vintage Fashion	2			Miss Sophie's

ACCOMMODATION	
Hostel Emma	4
Hotel 16 –	
U sv Kateřiny	6
Hotel Jungmann	1
Icon Hotel	2
Mánes	3
Miss Sophie's	5

CHURCH OF PANNA MARIA SNĚŽNÁ

Jungmannovo náměstí 18. MAP P.97, POCKET MAP H13

Once one of the great landmarks of Wenceslas Square, **Panna Maria Sněžná** (St Mary-of-the-Snows) is now barely visible from the surrounding streets. To reach the church, go through the archway behind the statue of Jungmann, and across the courtyard beyond. Founded in the fourteenth century as a Carmelite monastery by Emperor Charles IV, who envisaged a vast coronation church larger than St Vitus Cathedral, only the chancel was built before the money ran out. The result is curious – a church which is short in length, but equal to the cathedral in height. The 33m-high, prettily painted vaulting is awesome, as is the gargantuan gold and black Baroque main altar which almost touches the ceiling.

NÁRODNÍ

MAP P.97, POCKET MAP F14-G13

It was on this busy street, lined with shops, galleries and clubs, that the Velvet Revolution began. On **November 17, 1989**, a 50,000-strong student demonstration worked its way down Národní aiming to reach Wenceslas Square. Halfway

down the street their way was barred by the Communist riot-police. The students sat down and refused to disperse, some of them handing flowers out to the police. Suddenly, without any warning, the police attacked, and what became known as the *masakr* (massacre) began. In actual fact, no one was killed, though it wasn't for want of trying by the police. Under the arches of Národní 16, there's a small symbolic bronze relief of eight hands reaching out for help.

Further down Národní, on the right-hand side, is an eye-catching duo of Art Nouveau buildings. The first, at no. 7, was built for the **Prague Savings Bank (pojišťovna Praha)**, hence the beautiful mosaic lettering above the windows advertising *život* (life insurance) and *kapital* (loans), as well as help with your *důchod* (pension) and *věno* (dowry). Next door, the slightly more ostentatious **Topičův dům**, headquarters of the official state publishers, provides the perfect accompaniment, with a similarly ornate wrought-iron and glass canopy.

CAFÉ SLAVIA

Smetanovo nábřeží 2. Daily 8am–midnight, Sat & Sun from 9am. MAP P.97, POCKET MAP F13

The **Café Slavia** (see also p.104), opposite the National Theatre, has been a favourite haunt of the city's writers, dissidents, artists and actors since the 1920s when the Czech avant-garde movement, **Devětsil**, used to hold its meetings here, recorded for posterity by Nobel prize-winning poet Jaroslav Seifert. Under the Communists, dissident (and later president) Václav Havel and his pals used to hang out here. The ambience is not what it once was, but it still has a great riverside view and Viktor Oliva's classic *Absinthe Drinker* canvas on the wall.

STŘELECKÝ OSTROV (SHOOTERS' ISLAND)

Most Legií. MAP P.97, POCKET MAP E13–14

The **Střelecký ostrov** is where the army held their shooting practice, on and off, from the fifteenth until the nineteenth century. Closer to the other bank, and accessible via **most Legií** (Legion's Bridge), it became a favourite spot for a Sunday promenade, and is still popular, especially in summer. The first Sokol gymnastics festival was held here in 1882, and the first May Day demonstrations took place here in 1890.

NATIONAL THEATRE (NÁRODNÍ DIVADLO)

Národní 2 ⊕ www.narodni-divadlo.cz. MAP P.97, POCKET MAP F14

Overlooking the Vltava is the gold-crested **National Theatre**, proud symbol of the Czech nation. Refused money from the Habsburg state coffers, Czechs of all classes dug deep into their pockets to raise the funds. After thirteen years of construction, in June 1881, the theatre opened with a premiere of Smetana's *Libuše*. In August of the same year, fire ripped through the building, destroying everything except the outer walls. Within two years the whole thing was rebuilt and even the emperor contributed this time. The grand portal on the north side of the theatre is embellished with suitably triumphant allegorical figures, and, inside, every square centimetre is taken up with paintings and sculptures by leading artists of the Czech national revival.

Standing behind the old National Theatre, and in dramatic contrast with it, is the theatre's unattractive extension, the opaque glass box of the **Nová scéna**, completed in 1983. It's one of those buildings most Praguers love to hate, though compared to much of Prague's Communist-era architecture, it's not that bad. Just for the record, the lump of molten rock in the courtyard is a symbolic evocation entitled *My Socialist Country*.

VODIČKOVA

MAP P.97, POCKET MAP G14–H13

Vodičkova is probably the most impressive of the streets that head south from Wenceslas Square. Of the handful of buildings worth checking out on the way, the most remarkable is **U Nováků** with its mosaic of bucolic frolicking and its delicate, ivy-like wrought-ironwork – look out for the frog-prince holding up a windowsill. Further down the street stands the imposing neo-Renaissance **Minerva** girls' school, covered in bright red sgraffito. Founded in 1866, it was the first such institution in Prague, and notorious for the antics of its pupils, the "Minervans", who shocked bourgeois Czech society by experimenting with fashion, drugs and sexual freedom.

KARLOVO NÁMĚSTÍ

MAP P.97, POCKET MAP G15

Once Prague's biggest square, **Karlovo náměstí**'s impressive proportions are no longer so easy to appreciate, obscured by trees and cut in two by a busy thoroughfare. It was created by Emperor Charles IV as Nové Město's cattle market and used by him for the grisly annual public display of his impressive collection of saintly relics. Now it signals the southern limit of the city's main commercial district and the beginning of predominantly residential Nové Město.

NOVÉ MĚSTO TOWN HALL (NOVOMĚSTSKÁ RADNICE)

Karlovo náměstí 23 ⓦwww .nrpraha.cz. Easter to mid-Oct Tues–Sun 10am–6pm. 50Kč. MAP P.97, POCKET MAP G14

Built in the fourteenth century, the **Nové Město Town Hall** is one of the finest Gothic buildings in the city, sporting three impressive triangular gables embellished with intricate blind tracery. It was here that Prague's **first defenestration** took place on July 30, 1419, when the radical Hussite preacher Jan Želivský and his penniless religious followers stormed the building, mobbed the councillors and burghers, and threw twelve or thirteen of them (including the mayor) out of the town hall windows onto the pikes of the Hussite mob below, who clubbed any survivors to death. Václav IV, on hearing the news, suffered a stroke and died just two weeks later. So began the long and bloody Hussite Wars. After the amalgamation of Prague's separate towns in 1784, the building was used solely as a criminal court and prison. Nowadays, you can visit the site of the defenestration, and climb to the top of the tower for a view over central Prague. The town hall also puts on temporary art exhibitions.

CHURCH OF SV IGNÁC

Karlovo náměstí. MAP P.97, POCKET MAP G15
Begun in 1665, this former **Jesuit church** is quite remarkable inside, a pink and white confection, with lots of frothy stucco work and an exuberant pulpit dripping with gold drapery, cherubs and saints. The statue of St Ignatius, which sits above the entrance surrounded by a sunburst, caused controversy at the time, as until then only the Holy Trinity had been depicted in such a way.

CATHEDRAL OF SV CYRIL AND METODĚJ (HEYDRICH MARTYRS' MEMORIAL)

Resslova/Na Zderaze ⓦwww.pamatnik-heydrichiady.cz. March–Oct Tues–Sun 9am–5pm; Nov–Feb Tues–Sat 9am–5pm. 75Kč. MAP P.97, POCKET MAP F15
Amid all the traffic, it's extremely difficult to imagine the scene outside Prague's **Orthodox cathedral** on June 18, 1942, when seven Czechoslovak secret agents were besieged in the church by hundreds of SS troops. The agents had pulled off the dramatic assassination of Nazi leader **Reinhard Heydrich**, but had been betrayed by one of their own men. The Nazis surrounded the church just after 4am and fought a pitched battle for over six hours, trying explosives, flooding and any other method they could think of to drive the men out of their stronghold in the crypt. Eventually, all seven agents committed suicide rather than give themselves up. There's a plaque at street level on the south wall commemorating

those who died, and an exhibition inside – you can also visit the crypt itself, which has been left pretty much as it was.

SLOVANSKÝ OSTROV (SLAV ISLAND)

Masarykovo nábřeží. MAP P.97, POCKET MAP E14–F15
Slovanský ostrov is commonly known as **Žofín**, after the island's very yellow cultural centre, built in 1835 and named for Sophie, the mother of Emperor Franz-Josef I. By the late nineteenth century the island had become one of the city's foremost pleasure gardens, and even today concerts, balls and other social gatherings take place here. Rowing boats can be rented in the summer. At the island's southern tip stands the onion-domed **Šítek water tower** and, spanning the narrow channel between the island and the embankment, the **Mánes** art gallery, a striking, white functionalist box designed in 1930. At the northern end is a bronze of the best-known Czech female writer Božena Němcová.

SLOVANSKÝ OSTROV

DANCING HOUSE (TANČÍCÍ DŮM)

Rašínovo nábřeží 80. MAP P.97, POCKET MAP F15
Designed by Frank O. Gehry
and Vlado Milunič, this
building is known as the
Dancing House (Tančící dům)
or "Fred and Ginger building",
after the shape of the building's
two towers, which look vaguely
like a couple ballroom dancing.
The apartment block next door
was built at the start of the
twentieth century by Havel's
grandfather, and was where,
until the early 1990s, Havel and
his first wife, Olga, lived in the
top-floor flat.

PALACKÝ MONUMENT

Palackého náměstí. MAP P.97, POCKET MAP D7
The **Monument to František
Palacký**, the nineteenth-
century Czech historian,
politician and nationalist, is an
energetic and inspirational Art
Nouveau sculpture from 1912.
Ethereal bronze bodies,
representing the world of the
imagination, shoot out at all
angles, contrasting sharply
with the plain stone mass of
the plinth, and below, the giant
seated figure of Palacký,
representing the real world.

EMAUZY MONASTERY

Vyšehradská 49 ⓦ www.emauzy.cz. April–Oct
Mon–Sat 11am–5pm; Nov–March Mon–Fri
11am–2pm. 50Kč. MAP P.97, POCKET MAP D8
The intertwined concrete spires
of the **Emauzy monastery** are
an unusual modern addition to
the Prague skyline. The
monastery was one of the few
important historical buildings
to be damaged in World War
II, in this case by a stray
Anglo-American bomb (the
pilot thought he was over
Dresden). Founded by Emperor
Charles IV, the cloisters contain
some extremely valuable
Gothic frescoes.

DANCING HOUSE

Shops

BAZAR

Vyšehradská 8. Erratic opening hours. MAP P.97, POCKET MAP D8

This junk shop south of the city centre sells everything from socialist-era pin badges to 1960s lightshades, and from 1980s Czechoslovak toy cars to German-built wardrobes.

GLOBE

Pštrossova 6. Mon–Fri 10am–midnight, Sat & Sun 9.30am–1am. MAP P.97, POCKET MAP F15

The expat bookshop *par excellence* – both a social centre and superbly well-stocked store with friendly staff.

GOLD PRALINES

V jámě 1. Daily 9am–8pm. MAP P.97, POCKET MAP H14

Top-quality Belgian chocolates – make sure you try the uniquely Czech pralines filled with the national *digestif*, Becherovka.

JAN PAZDERA

Vodičkova 28. Mon–Fri 10am–6pm, Sat 10am–1pm. MAP P.97, POCKET MAP H14

Truly spectacular selection of old and new cameras, microscopes, telescopes, opera glasses and binoculars.

KRAKATIT

Jungmannova 14. Mon–Fri 9.30am–6pm, Sat 9.30am–1pm. MAP P.97, POCKET MAP G13

This is big boys' nirvana – a little shop stuffed with fantasy and military literature including science fiction, fantasy and comics.

MPM

Myslíkova 19. Mon–Fri 9am–6pm, Sat 9am–1pm. MAP P.97, POCKET MAP F15

A whole range of kits for making model planes, tanks, trains, ships and cars, and toy soldiers.

GLOBE

MY NÁRODNÍ

Národní 26. Mon–Sat 8am–9pm, Sun 9am–8pm. MAP P.97, POCKET MAP G13

My Národní is Prague's premier downtown department store. The name is a pun on its Communist predecessor (called Máj), and it's actually owned by the British supermarket chain Tesco, as the basement food hall attests.

PYLONES

28. října 11. Mon–Sat 10am–8pm, Sun 10am–7pm. MAP P.97 POCKET MAP H13

More like a museum of the wacky, *Pylones* is filled with colourful gizmos and gadgets for the office or home.

QUASIMODO VINTAGE FASHION

Vladislavova 17. Mon–Fri 10am–6pm. MAP P.97, POCKET MAP G13

This good secondhand store is hidden away in an attractive courtyard. The clothes and accessories here are not exclusively vintage, more plain old secondhand, and all the more affordable for it, with pieces selling for around 200–400Kč.

Cafés

CAFÉ 35 – INSTITUT FRANÇAIS

Štěpánská 35. Mon–Fri 8.30am–8.30pm, Sat 9.30am–3.30pm. MAP P.97, POCKET MAP H14
Housed in Prague's Institut Français, you can be sure of great coffee and fresh pastries – plus the chance to pose with a French newspaper.

CAFÉ LOUVRE

Národní 22. Mon–Fri 8am–11.30pm, Sat & Sun 9am–11.30pm. MAP P.97, POCKET MAP G13
Swish, turn-of-the-twentieth-century café with a long pedigree, and still a popular stop for shoppers. There are high ceilings, mirrors, daily papers, inexpensive food and cakes, a billiard hall and window seats overlooking Národní, but also a large smoking area not divided from the rest of the dining area.

CAFÉ SLAVIA

Smetanovo nábřeží 2. Mon–Fri 8am–midnight, Sat & Sun 9am–midnight. MAP P.97, POCKET MAP F13
This famous 1920s riverside café pulls in a mixed crowd from shoppers and tourists to old-timers and the pre- and post-theatre mob. Come here for a coffee and the view, not the food or the service.

MARATHON

FRIENDS COFFEE HOUSE

Palackého 7. Mon–Fri 11am–10pm, Sat & Sun 2–10pm. MAP P.97, POCKET MAP H14
Big, popular, non-smoking café with great coffee, fresh sandwiches and other light snacks – one to linger in.

MARATHON

Černá 9. Mon–Fri 10am–midnight, Sat 6pm–midnight. MAP P.97, POCKET MAP G14
Smoky, self-styled "library café" in the university's 1920s-style religious faculty, hidden in the backstreets, south of Národní.

ST TROPEZ

Vodičkova 30. Mon–Fri 8am–8pm, Sat 9am–7pm, Sun 10am–7pm. MAP P.97, POCKET MAP H14
Light and airy, family-run French patisserie inside the U Nováků building on Vodičkova.

SVATOVÁCLAVSKÁ CUKRÁRNA

Václavská pasáž, Karlovo náměstí 6. Mon–Fri 8am–7pm, Sat & Sun 9am–7pm. MAP P.97, POCKET MAP D7
Join the local pensioner posse for cheap Turkish coffee and a slice of strudel at this busy *cukrárna* (café-bakery) within the glass-roofed Václavská pasáž, an interwar shopping arcade well off the tourist trail.

VELRYBA (THE WHALE)

Opatovická 24. Mon–Fri 11am–midnight, Sat 5pm–midnight. MAP P.97, POCKET MAP G14
Long-established, grungy but authentic hippy-student hangout opposite the Church of sv Michala serving Žatec beer, cheap pastas and lots of meat (mains 100–220Kč).

Restaurants

CICALA

Žitná 43 ☎ 222 210 375. Mon–Sat 11.30am–10pm. MAP P.97, POCKET MAP H15
Very good family-run Italian basement restaurant

specializing (mid-week) in fresh seafood (from 300Kč). There's also a wide range of pasta (110–260Kč) and an appetizing antipasto selection.

DYNAMO

Pštrossova 29 ☎ 224 932 020. Daily 11.30am–midnight. MAP P.97, POCKET MAP F14
Fashionable little spot with eye-catching retro-1960s designer decor, tapas, vegetarian and pasta dishes (150–190Kč), and steaks and Czech dishes for around 200Kč.

MISS SAIGON

Myslíkova 26 ☎ 222 560 328, ⊛ www.miss -saigon.cz. Mon–Fri 10.30am–11pm, Sat & Sun 11.30am–11pm. MAP P.97, POCKET MAP G14
The Czech Republic has a large Vietnamese population who moved here during the Communist period, but their cuisine is virtually unknown here. This simple place tries to put this right with a menu of exotic ingredients (bamboo shoots, oyster sauce, cashew nuts, bean curd) and the staple dish – *pho bo* soup. Mains 140–270Kč.

PIZZERIA KMOTRA (GODMOTHER)

V jirchářích 12 ☎ 224 934 100. Daily 11am–midnight. MAP P.97, POCKET MAP F14
This inexpensive, brick-vaulted basement pizza place is popular, and justifiably so – if possible, book a table in advance. Pizzas 125–160Kč.

POSEZENÍ U ČIRINY

Navrátilova 6 ☎ 222 231 709. Mon–Sat 11am–11pm. MAP P.97, POCKET MAP G14
Little family-run place, with only a handful of tables inside, leather benches in cosy alcoves, and a summer terrace. Classic Slovak home cooking for around 230Kč, including national dish *Bryndzové halušky*, similar to gnocchi with sheep's cheese.

DYNAMO

RENOMMÉ

Na sturze 1 ☎ 224 934 109. Daily 11am–11pm. MAP P.97, POCKET MAP F14
Around the corner from the National Theatre, this elegant little family-run restaurant serves delicious, beautiful treats. Foie gras and fresh fish are two of their specialities (190–390Kč).

STŘELECKÝ OSTROV

Střelecký ostrov 336 ☎ 606 750 006. Daily 11am–11pm. MAP P.97, POCKET MAP E14
The kitchen here serves up classic Czech cuisine (mains from around 300Kč), but it's the location – on an island in the Vltava, with a terrace overlooking the National Theatre – that's the big draw.

ŽOFÍN GARDEN

Slovanský ostrov 226 ☎ 774 774 774. Mon– Sat 11am–10pm, Sun 11am–3pm & 5–10pm. MAP P.97, POCKET MAP E14
With a superb riverside location on the island nearest the National Theatre, *Žofín* serves up beautifully presented pizzas and pasta, barbecued fish, tiger prawns and rib-eye steak (200–350Kč).

Pubs

BRANICKÝ SKLÍPEK

Vodičkova 26. Mon–Fri 10am–11pm, Sat & Sun 11am–11pm. MAP P.97, POCKET MAP H14
Convenient downtown pub (aka *U Purkmistra*) decked out like a pine furniture showroom serving typical Czech dishes and jugs of Prague's Braník beer. The rough-and-ready *Branická formanka* next door opens and closes earlier.

NOVOMĚSTSKÝ PIVOVAR

Vodičkova 20 ⓦ www.npivovar.cz. Mon–Fri 10am–11.30pm, Sat 11.30am–11.30pm, Sun noon–10pm. MAP P.97, POCKET MAP G14
Outstanding microbrewery which serves its own 11° home brew, plus huge portions of Czech food, in twelve sprawling beer halls and rooms, some underground Gothic affairs.

PIVOVARKSÝ DŮM

Corner of Lipová/ Ječná. Daily 11am–11.30pm. MAP P.97, POCKET MAP H15
Busy microbrewery dominated by big, shiny copper vats, serving gorgeous light, mixed and dark unfiltered beer (plus banana, coffee and wheat varieties), and Czech pub dishes.

PIVOVARKSÝ DŮM

U FLEKŮ

Křemencova 11. Daily 10am–11pm. MAP P.97, POCKET MAP F14
Famous medieval brewery where the unique dark 13° beer, Flek, has been brewed since 1499. Seats over five hundred at a go, serves short measures (0.4l), charges extra for the music and still you might have to queue. Visit just to sample the beer, which you're best off doing during the day.

U HAVRANA (THE CROW)

Hálkova 6. Mon–Fri 5pm–5am, Sat 6pm–5am. MAP P.97 POCKET MAP J15
The chief virtue of this ordinary and surprisingly unseedy Czech pub is that it serves food and Velkopopovický kozel beer until the wee hours.

U KRUHU (THE WHEEL)

Palackého 21. Daily 11am–10pm. MAP P.97, POCKET MAP H14
Proper Czech pub, serving Plzeň beers and Velkopovický kozel, with its own garden courtyard out front.

U PINKASŮ

Jungmannovo náměstí 16. Daily 10am–3.30am. MAP P.97, POCKET MAP H13
Famous as the pub where Pilsner Urquell was first served in Prague, it still serves excellent unpasteurized beer and classic Czech pub food.

VÝLOHA BAR

Vyšehradská 12 ☎ 606 762 022, ⓦ www .vylohabar.cz. Mon–Thurs 5pm–1am, Fri & Sat 5pm–2am, Sun 5pm–midnight. MAP P.97, POCKET MAP D8
At the southern end of the Nové Město, this neighbourhood bar is great for hanging with locals, playing darts and watching the Czechs win at ice hockey. Next door to Prague's Toilet Museum.

Clubs and venues

DIVADLO MINOR

Vodičkova 6 📞 222 231 351, 🌐 www.minor.cz.
MAP P.97, POCKET MAP G14

The former state puppet theatre puts on children's shows most days, plus adult shows on occasional evenings, sometimes with English subtitles.

EVALD

Národní 28 📞 221 105 225, 🌐 www.evald.cz.
MAP P.97, POCKET MAP G13

Prague's most centrally located arthouse cinema shows a discerning selection of new releases interspersed with plenty of classics.

LATERNA MAGIKA (MAGIC LANTERN)

Nová scéna, Národní 4 📞 224 901 417, 🌐 www.narodni-divadlo.cz. MAP P.97, POCKET MAP F14

The National Theatre's Nová scéna, one of Prague's most modern and versatile stages, is the main base for Laterna magika, founders of multimedia and "black light" theatre in 1958. Their slick productions continue effortlessly to pull in crowds of curious tourists.

MAT STUDIO

Karlovo náměstí 19, entrance on Odborů 📞 224 915 765, 🌐 www.mat.cz. MAP P.97, POCKET MAP G15

Tiny café and cinema popular with the film crowd, with an eclectic programme of shorts, documentaries and Czech films with English subtitles.

NATIONAL THEATRE (NÁRODNÍ DIVADLO)

Národní 2 📞 224 901 448, 🌐 www.narodni-divadlo.cz. MAP P.97, POCKET MAP F14

The living embodiment of the Czech national revival

NATIONAL THEATRE

movement, the National Theatre is worth visiting for the decor alone. Czech plays are core to the repertoire; there's also ballet and English-subtitled opera.

NEBE (HEAVEN)

Křemencova 10 🌐 www.nebepraha.cz. Mon 4pm–3am, Tues–Thurs 4pm–4am, Fri & Sat 4pm–5am, Sun 6pm–3am. MAP P.97, POCKET MAP F14

A simple formula: a snaking, brick-vaulted cocktail bar with a long ethnol-based menu and DJs that pump out dance music from the last three or four decades. Cover charge 80–150Kč.

REDUTA

Národní 20 📞 224 933 487, 🌐 www.redutajazzclub.cz. Daily from 9.30pm.
MAP P.97, POCKET MAP G13

Prague's best-known jazz club – Bill Clinton played his sax here in front of Havel – attracts a touristy crowd, but also some decent acts.

ROCK CAFÉ

Národní 20 🌐 www.rockcafe.cz. Mon–Fri 10am–3am, Sat 5pm–3am, Sun 5pm–1am.
MAP P.97, POCKET MAP G13

Not to be confused with the *Hard Rock Café*, this place is a stalwart of the live music scene; the basement stage showcases mostly new Czech bands. Admission 100–150Kč.

107

Vyšehrad, Vinohrady and Žižkov

The fortress of Vyšehrad makes for a perfect afternoon escape away from the human congestion of the city centre: its cemetery shelters the remains of Bohemia's artistic elite; the ramparts afford superb views over the river; and below the fortress there are several interesting examples of Czech Cubist architecture. Vinohrady, to the east, is a late nineteenth-century residential suburb, dominated by long streets of grandiose apartment blocks, with one or two specific sights to guide your wandering. By contrast, Žižkov, further north, is a grittier working-class district, whose shabby, run-down streets contain many pubs and clubs.

CUBIST VILLAS

MAP OPPOSITE, POCKET MAP D8

Even if you harbour only a passing interest in modern architecture, it's worth seeking out the cluster of **Cubist villas** below the fortress in Vyšehrad. The most impressive example is the apartment block at **Neklanova 30**, begun in 1913, which brilliantly exploits its angular location. Further along Neklanova, at no. 2, there's another Cubist facade, and around the corner is the most ambitious of the lot, the **Kovařovicova vila**, which uses prism shapes and angular lines to produce the sharp geometric contrasts of light and dark shadows characteristic of Cubist painting.

KOVAŘOVICOVA VILA, LIBUŠINA 49

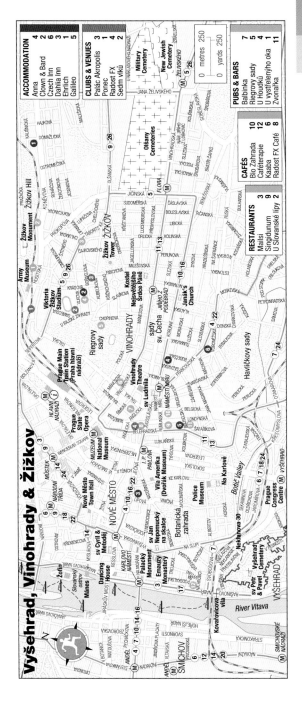

Vyšehrad, Vinohrady & Žižkov

ACCOMMODATION

Anna	4
Clown & Bard	6
Czech Inn	2
Dahlia Inn	3
Ehrlich	1
Galileo	5

CLUBS & VENUES

Palác Akropolis	3
Ponec	1
Radost FX	4
Sedm vlků	2

CAFÉS

Bio Zahrada	10
Caféterapie	9
Kaaba	6
Radost FX Café	8

RESTAURANTS

Mailsi	3
Singidunum	9
U Slovanské lípy	2

PUBS & BARS

Balbínka	7
Riegrovy sady	5
U Houdků	4
U vystřelenýho oka	1
Zvonařka	11

0 metres 250
0 yards 250

VYŠEHRAD

V pevnosti 5b ⓦwww.praha-vysehrad.cz. Open 24hr. Free. MAP P.109, POCKET MAP D9

The rocky red-brick fortress of **Vyšehrad** – literally "High Castle" – has more myths attached to it than any other place in Bohemia. According to Czech legend, this is the place where the Slav tribes first settled in Prague and where the "wise and tireless chieftain" Krok built a castle, whence his youngest daughter Libuše went on to found Praha itself. Alas, the archeological evidence doesn't really bear this claim out. What you see now are the remains of a fortified barracks built by the Habsburgs and then turned into a public park.

You can explore the fortress's northern entrance, or **Cihelná brána** (daily: April–Oct 9.30am–6pm; Nov–March 9.30am–5pm; free), and the adjacent **dungeons** or *kasematy* (same hours; 60Kč). After a short guided tour of a section of the underground passageways underneath the ramparts, you enter a vast storage hall, which shelters several of the original statues from Charles Bridge, and, when the lights are switched

CIHELNÁ BRÁNA, VYŠEHRAD

off, reveals a camera obscura image of a tree.

Over in the southwestern corner of the fortress, in the **Gothic cellar** (same hours; 50Kč), there's also a permanent exhibition on the history of Vyšehrad. The rock's big moment in Czech history was in the eleventh century when Přemysl Vratislav II – the first Bohemian ruler to bear the title "king" – built a royal palace here to get away from his younger brother who was lording it in the Hrad. Within half a century the royals had moved back to Hradčany, into a new palace, and from then on Vyšehrad began to lose its political significance.

CHURCH OF SV PETR AND PAVEL

K rotundě 10. Tues–Sat 10am–4pm, Sun 10.30am–4pm. 50Kč. MAP P.109, POCKET MAP D9

The twin open-work spires of this blackened sandstone church, rebuilt in the 1880s in neo-Gothic style on the site of an eleventh-century basilica, are now the fortress's most familiar landmark. Inside, you can admire the church's **Art Nouveau murals**, which cover just about every available surface.

To reach Vyšehrad, take tram #3, #7 or #17 to Výtoň, and either wind your way up Vratislavova to the Cihelná brána or take the steep stairway from Rašínovo nábřeží that leads up through the trees. Alternatively, from Vyšehrad metro station, walk west past the ugly Prague Congress Centre, and enter via V pevnosti, where there's an information centre (daily: April–Oct 9.30am–6pm; Nov–March 9.30am–5pm).

DOORS OF THE CHURCH OF SV PETR AND PAVEL

Ladislav Šaloun's grave for **Dvořák**, situated under the arches, is one of the more showy ones, with a mosaic inscription, studded with gold stones, glistening behind wrought-iron railings. **Smetana**, who died twenty years earlier, is buried in comparatively modest surroundings near the **Slavín monument**, the cemetery's focal point, which is the communal resting place of more than fifty Czech artists, including the painter Alfons Mucha and the opera singer Ema Destinová. The grave of the Romantic poet Karel Hynek Mácha was the assembly point for the demonstration on November 17, 1989, which triggered the Velvet Revolution. This was organized to commemorate the fiftieth anniversary of the Nazi closure of Czech higher education institutions. A 50,000-strong crowd gathered here and attempted to march to Wenceslas Square, getting as far as Národní before being beaten back (see p.98).

VYŠEHRAD CEMETERY (VYŠEHRADSKÝ HŘBITOV)

📶 www.slavin.cz. Daily: May–Sept 8am–7pm; Oct 8am–6pm; Nov–April 8am–5pm. Free. MAP P.109, POCKET MAP D9

Most Czechs come to Vyšehrad to pay a visit to the **cemetery**. It's a measure of the part that artists and intellectuals played in the foundation of the nation, and the regard in which they are still held, that the most prestigious graveyard in the city is given over to them: no soldiers, no politicians – not even the Communists managed to muscle their way in here (except on artistic merit). Sheltered from the wind by its high walls, lined on two sides by delicate arcades, it's a tiny cemetery filled with well-kept graves, many of them designed by the country's leading sculptors.

To the uninitiated only a handful of figures are well known, but for the Czechs the place is alive with great names (there's a useful plan of the most notable graves at the entrance nearest the church).

VYŠEHRAD CEMETERY

VILA AMERIKA

POLICE MUSEUM

Ke Karlovu 1, Ⓜ Karlovo náměstí. Tues–Sun 10am–5pm. 30Kč. MAP P.109, POCKET MAP E8

The former Augustinian monastery of Karlov houses the **Police Museum**, which concentrates on road and traffic offences, and the force's latest challenges: forgery, drugs and murder. There's a whole section on the old Iron Curtain and espionage, but not a huge amount of information in English. If you've got kids, however, they might enjoy driving round the mini-road layout on one of the museum trikes.

NA KARLOVĚ CHURCH

Ke Karlovu, Ⓜ Karlovo náměstí. No set hours. Free. MAP P.109, POCKET MAP E8

Founded by Emperor Charles IV and designed in imitation of Charlemagne's tomb in Aachen, this octagonal church is quite unlike any other in Prague. If it's open, you should take a look at the dark interior, which was remodelled in the sixteenth century by Bonifaz Wohlmut. The stellar vault has no central supporting pillars – a remarkable feat of engineering for its time, and one which gave rise to numerous legends about the architect being in league with the Devil.

VILA AMERIKA (DVOŘÁK MUSEUM)

Ke Karlovu 20, Ⓜ I. P. Pavlova. Tues–Sun 10am–1.30pm & 2–5pm. 50Kč. MAP P.109, POCKET MAP E7

The russet-coloured **Vila Amerika** was originally named after the local pub, but is now a museum devoted to **Antonín Dvořák** (1841–1904), the most famous of all Czech composers, who lived for a time on nearby Zitná. Even if you've no interest in Dvořák, the villa itself is a delight, built as a Baroque summer house from around 1720. The tasteful period rooms, with the composer's music wafting in and out, and the tiny garden dotted with Baroque sculptures, together go a long way towards compensating for what the display cabinets may lack.

NÁMĚSTÍ MÍRU

MAP P.109, POCKET MAP F7

If Vinohrady has a centre, it's
the leafy square of **náměstí
Míru**, a good introduction to
this neighbourhood. The most
flamboyant building here is the
Vinohrady Theatre (Divadlo
na Vinohradech), built in 1907,
with both Art Nouveau and
neo-Baroque elements. At the
centre of the square stands the
brick basilica of **sv Ludmila**,
designed in the late 1880s in a
severe neo-Gothic style, though
the interior has the odd
flourish of Art Nouveau. In
front a statue commemorates
the **Čapek brothers**, writer
Karel and painter Josef, local
residents who together
symbolized the golden era of
the interwar republic. Karel
died of pneumonia in 1938,
while Josef perished in Belsen
seven years later.

KOSTEL NEJSVĚTĚJŠÍHO SRDCE
PÁNĚ

Náměstí Jiřího z Poděbrad, Ⓜ Jiřího z
Poděbrad. No set hours. Free. MAP P.109, POCKET
MAP G7

Prague's most celebrated
modern church, **Nejsvětějšího
Srdce Páně** (Chruch of the
Most Holy Heart of Our Lord)
was built in 1928 by the Slovene
architect **Josip Plečnik**. It's a
marvellously eclectic work,
employing a sophisticated
potpourri of architectural styles:
a Neoclassical pediment and a
great slab of a clock tower with
a giant transparent face in
imitation of a Gothic rose
window, as well as the bricks
and mortar of contemporary
constructivism. Plečnik also had
a sharp eye for detail; look out
for the little gold crosses inset
into the brickwork like stars,
inside and out, and the celestial
orbs of light suspended above
the congregation.

ŽIŽKOV TOWER (TELEVIZNÍ VĚŽ)

Mahlerovy sady 1, Ⓜ Jiřího z Poděbrad.
Ⓦ www.towerpark.cz. Daily 8am–midnight.
180Kč. MAP P.109, POCKET MAP G6

At 216m in height, the Žižkov
TV tower is the tallest building
in Prague. Close up, it's an
intimidating futuristic piece of
architecture, made all the more
disturbing by the giant babies
crawling up the sides, courtesy
of artist **David Černý**. Begun
in the 1970s in a desperate bid
to jam West German television
transmissions, the tower
became fully operational only
in the 1990s. In the course of
its construction, however, the
Communists saw fit to
demolish part of a nearby
Jewish cemetery that had
served the community between
1787 and 1891; a small section
survives to the northwest of the
tower. Following a major
reconstruction, the tower now
features a café, restaurant, bar,
observatory and even a
one-room hotel.

ŽIŽKOV TV TOWER

OLŠANY CEMETERIES (OLŠANSKÉ HŘBITOVY)

Vinohradská, ⓂFlora. Daily dawn–dusk. Free. MAP P.109, POCKET MAP H6–J6

The vast Olšany cemeteries were originally created for the victims of the great plague epidemic of 1680. The perimeter walls are lined with glass cabinets, stacked like shoe-boxes, containing funereal urns and mementos, while the graves themselves are a mixed bag of artistic achievements, reflecting the funereal fashions of the day as much as the character of the deceased. The cemeteries are divided into districts and crisscrossed with cobbled streets; at each gate there's a map and an aged janitor ready to point you in the right direction.

The cemeteries' two most famous incumbents are an ill-fitting couple: **Klement Gottwald**, the country's first Communist president, whose remains were removed from the mausoleum on Žižkov hill after 1989 and reinterred here; and **Jan Palach**, the philosophy student who set light to himself in January 1969 in protest at the Soviet occupation. More than 750,000 people attended Palach's funeral, and in an attempt to put a stop to the annual vigils at his graveside, the secret police removed his body and reburied him in his home town outside Prague. In 1990, Palach's body was returned to Olšany; you'll find it just to the east of the main entrance.

NEW JEWISH CEMETERY (NOVÝ ŽIDOVSKÝ HŘBITOV)

Izraelská 1, ⓂŽelivského. April–Oct Mon–Thurs & Sun 9am–5pm, Fri 9am–2pm; Nov–March Mon–Thurs & Sun 9am–4pm, Fri 9am–2pm. 50Kč. MAP P.109, POCKET MAP K6

Founded in the 1890s, the **New Jewish Cemetery** was designed to last for a century, with room for 100,000 graves. It's a truly melancholy spot, particularly in the east of the cemetery, where large empty allotments wait in vain to be filled by the generation that perished in the Holocaust. Most people come here to visit **Franz Kafka's grave**, which is located 400m east along the south wall and signposted from the entrance. He is buried, along with his mother and father (both of whom outlived him), beneath a plain headstone; the plaque below is dedicated to the memory of his three sisters, who died in the concentration camps.

GRAVESTONE AT OLŠANY

ŽIŽKOV HILL

U památníku, bus #133, #175 or #207 from Ⓜ Florenc. MAP P.109, POCKET MAP G5–H5

Žižkov Hill is the thin green wedge of land that separates Žižkov from Karlín, the grid-plan industrial district to the north. From its western-most point, which juts out almost to the edge of Nové Město, is the definitive panoramic view over the city centre. It was here, on July 14, 1420, that the Hussites enjoyed their first and finest victory at the **Battle of Vítkov**, under the inspired leadership of the one-eyed general, Jan Žižka (hence the name of the district). Outnumbered by ten to one, Žižka and his fanatical troops thoroughly trounced the Bohemian king (and Holy Roman Emperor Sigismund) and his papal forces.

Despite its totalitarian aesthetics, the giant concrete **Žižkov monument**, which graces the crest of the hill, was actually built between the wars as a memorial to the Czecho-slovak Legion who fought against the Habsburgs in World War I – the gargantuan statue of the mace-wielding Žižka, which fronts the monument, is reputedly the world's largest equestrian statue. The building was later used by the Nazis as an arsenal, and eventually became a Communist mausoleum. In 1990, the Communists were cremated and quietly reinterred in Olšany. The monument now houses a fascinating **museum** (Ⓦ www.nm.cz; April–Oct Wed–Sun 10am–6pm; Nov–March Thurs–Sun 10am–6pm; 120Kč) on the country's twentieth-century history, a Communist monument to the fallen of World War II, and a café on top, with great views over Prague's suburbs.

ARMY MUSEUM (ARMÁDNÍ MUZEUM)

U památníku 2, bus #133, #175 or #207 from Ⓜ Florenc Ⓦ www.vhu.cz. Tues–Sun 10am–6pm. Free. MAP P.109, POCKET MAP G5

Guarded by a handful of unmanned tanks, howitzers and armoured vehicles, the **Army Museum** has a permanent exhibition covering the country's military history from 1914 to 1945. A fairly evenly balanced account of both world wars includes coverage of controversial subjects such as the exploits of the Czechoslovak Legion, the Heydrich assassination and the 1945 Prague Uprising.

Cafés

BIO ZAHRADA

Belgická 33. Mon–Thurs 8.30am–9pm, Fri 8.30am–10pm, Sat 10am–8pm. MAP P.109 POCKET MAP F7

Popular organic food store and café with a glorious back garden for warmer weather. Good coffee, organic breakfasts, and a lunch menu for around 130Kč.

CAFÉTERAPIE

Na hrobci 3. Mon–Fri 8.30am–10pm, Sat 9am–10pm, Sun 10am–10pm. MAP P.109, POCKET MAP D8

Small, simply furnished café that serves up nice healthy Mediterranean-influenced salads, sandwiches, toasties and a few hot dishes.

KAABA

Mánesova 20. Mon–Fri 8am–10pm, Sat 9am–10pm, Sun 10am–10pm. MAP P.109, POCKET MAP K14

This stylish ice-cream parlour of a café attracts a young trendy crowd with its mismatched 1950s repro chairs and tables. Serves breakfast, sandwiches, salads, soup and toasties.

RADOST FX CAFÉ

Bělehradská 120. Mon–Sat 11am–11pm, Sun 11am–4pm. MAP P.109, POCKET MAP J15

The veggie dishes at this expat favourite are filling (most

under 200Kč), and there's a weekend brunch, decadent decor and a dance soundtrack with live DJs at the weekend. However, it can be a disappointing culinary experience.

Restaurants

MAILSI

Lipanská 1 ☎ 222 717 783. Daily noon–3pm & 6–11pm. MAP P.109, POCKET MAP G6

Prague's only Pakistani restaurant is a friendly, unpretentious Punjabi place with great *tandoor* specialities for around 350Kč (as hot as you can handle). The decor includes a wall of aquariums.

SINGIDUNUM

Bělehradská 92 ☎ 222 544 113, Ⓦ www .singidunum.cz. Daily 9am–11pm. MAP P.109, POCKET MAP F7

Singidunum is the Latin for Belgrade, and it's the hot-tempered cuisine of the Balkans you'll find at this atmospheric place. There are *čevapčiči* (kebabs), Adriatic pastas, Croatian *pršut* (ham) plus Macedonian and Montenegran wines. Mains 100–300Kč.

U SLOVANSKÉ LÍPY

Tachovské náměstí 6, Žižkov ☎ 734 743 094, Ⓦ www.uslovanskelipy.cz. Daily 11am– midnight. MAP P.109, POCKET MAP H5

Žižkov's oldest tavern serves solid, no-nonsense Prague and Bohemian dishes in a wood-panelled dining room. Interesting guest ales on tap. Mains around 150Kč.

Pubs and bars

BALBINKA

Balbínova 6. Mon–Fri 5pm–midnight, Sat & Sun 6pm–midnight. MAP P.109, POCKET MAP K15

This small "poet's" pub is

RADOST FX CAFÉ

cherished by its regulars, and rightly so. With nightly live music ranging from rock to country or folk, part of the charm is never knowing what you might encounter.

RIEGROVY SADY

Riegrovy sady. Daily 11am–11pm. MAP P.109, POCKET MAP G6

A real slice of local life, a neighbourhood park café-pub whose beer terrace is perennially popular, especially for big TV sports events.

U HOUDKŮ

Bořivojova 110. Daily 11am–midnight. MAP P.109, POCKET MAP G6

Friendly local pub in the heart of Žižkov with a beer garden, Kozel on tap and cheap Czech food.

U VYSTŘELENÝHO OKA (THE SHOT-OUT EYE)

U božích bojovníků 3. Mon–Sat 4.30pm–1am. MAP P.109, POCKET MAP G5

Big, loud, heavy-drinking pub with good (sometimes live) indie rock and lashings of Měšťan beer, plus absinthe chasers.

ZVONAŘKA (THE BELL)

Šafaříkova 1. Mon–Thurs 11.30am–midnight, Fri 11.30am–1am, Sat noon–midnight, Sun noon–11pm; closed Sun Nov–March. MAP P.109, POCKET MAP F8

The smart modern pub has a summer terrace with great views over the Nuselské schody and Botič valley.

Clubs and venues

PALÁC AKROPOLIS

Kubelíkova 27 ☎ 296 330 913, Ⓦ www .palacakropolis.cz. Mon–Thurs 11am–12.30am, Fri 11am–1.30am, Sat & Sun 3pm–12.30am. MAP P.109, POCKET MAP G6

This old Art Deco theatre is Žižkov's most popular club venue – it's also a great place to just have a drink or a bite to eat, as well as checking out the DJ nights or the live gigs. Cover charge 100Kč and upwards for events.

PONEC

Husitská 24a ☎ 222 721 531, Ⓦ www .divadloponec.cz. MAP P.109, POCKET MAP G5

Former cinema, now an innovative dance venue and centre for the annual Tanec Praha dance festival in June.

RADOST FX

Bělehradská 120 ☎ 224 254 776, Ⓦ www .radostfx.cz. Thurs–Sat 10pm–4am. MAP P.109, POCKET MAP J15

This spacious club is Prague's longest-running all-round dance venue, with house and techno keeping the expats happy. Up to 250Kč entrance depending on the night.

SEDM VLKŮ (SEVEN WOLVES)

Vlkova 33 ☎ 222 711 725. Mon–Sat 5pm–3am. MAP P.109, POCKET MAP G6

Club-bar with a penchant for reggae, hard house, techno and drum'n'bass whose resident DJs make the most of the impressive sound system.

PONEC

Holešovice

Tucked into a U-bend in the River Vltava, the late nineteenth-century suburb of Holešovice boasts two huge splodges of green: Letná, overlooking the city centre, and, to the north, Stromovka, Prague's largest public park, bordering the Výstaviště funfair and trade fair grounds. A stroll through the park brings you to the Baroque chateau of Troja and the leafy zoo. Two important art museums are located in Holešovice – the city's main museum of modern art, Veletržní Palace, and the Dox Centre for Contemporary Art. Few tourists make it out here, but it's worth the effort, if only to remind yourself that Prague doesn't begin and end at Charles Bridge.

LETNÁ

MAP OPPOSITE, POCKET MAP D4

A high plateau hovering above the city, the flat green expanse of the **Letná** plain has long been the traditional assembly point for invading and besieging armies. Under the Communists, it was used primarily for the annual May Day parades, during which thousands trudged past the Sparta Prague stadium, where the Communist leaders would salute from their giant red podium. It once boasted the largest **Stalin monument** in the world: a 30m-high granite sculpture portraying a procession of Czechs and Russians being led to Communism by the Pied Piper figure of Stalin, but popularly dubbed *tlačenice* (the crush) because of its resemblance to a Communist-era bread queue. The monument was unveiled on May 1, 1955, but within a year Khrushchev had denounced Stalin, and the monument was blown up in 1962. On the site of the Stalin statue, overlooking the Vltava, stands a symbolic giant red **metronome** (which is lit up at night).

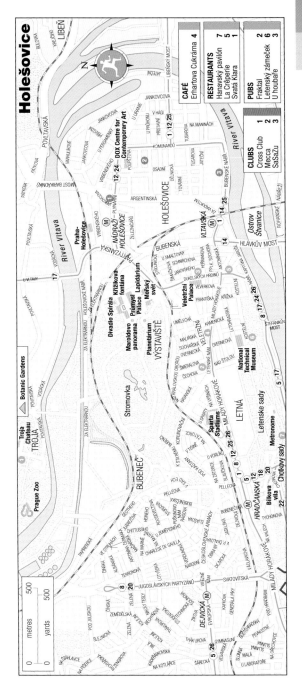

Holešovice

CAFÉ
Erhartova Cukrárna	4

RESTAURANTS
Hanavský pavilón	7
La Crêperie	5
Svatá Klara	1

PUBS
Fraktal	2
Letenský zámeček	6
U houbaře	3

CLUBS
Cross Club	1
Mecca	2
SaSaZu	3

SCULPTURE BY FRANTIŠEK BÍLEK, BÍLKOVA VILA

BÍLKOVA VILA

Mieckiewiczova 1 ⓦ www.ghmp.cz. Tues–Sun 10am–6pm. 120Kč. MAP P.119, POCKET MAP C4

The **Bílkova vila** honours one of the most original of all Czech sculptors, **František Bílek** (1872–1941). Built in 1911 to the artist's own design, the house was intended as both a "cathedral of art" and the family home. Inside, Bílek's extravagant religious sculptures line the walls of his "workshop and temple". In addition to his sculptural and relief work in wood and stone, often wildly expressive and spiritually tortured, there are also ceramics, graphics and a few mementoes of Bílek's life. His living quarters have also been restored and have much of the original wooden furniture, designed and carved by Bílek himself, still in place. Check out the dressing table for his wife, shaped like some giant church lectern, and the wardrobe decorated with a border of hearts, a penis, a nose, an ear and an eye plus the sun, stars and moon.

CHOTKOVY SADY

MAP P.119, POCKET MAP C4

Prague's first public park, the **Chotkovy sady**, was founded in 1833 by the ecologically minded city governor, Count Chotek. The atmosphere here is relaxed and you can happily stretch out on the grass and soak up the sun, or head for the south wall, for an unrivalled view of the bridges and islands of the Vltava. At the centre of the park there's a bizarre, melodramatic grotto-like memorial to the nineteenth-century Romantic poet **Julius Zeyer**, an elaborate monument from which life-sized characters from Zeyer's works, carved in white marble, emerge from the blackened rocks.

NATIONAL TECHNICAL MUSEUM (NÁRODNÍ TECHNICKÉ MUZEUM)

Kostelní 42 ⓦ www.ntm.cz. Tues–Fri 9am–5.30pm, Sat & Sun 10am–6pm. 190Kč. MAP P.119, POCKET MAP E4

Despite its dull name, this museum is surprisingly interesting, with a showpiece hangar-like main hall containing an impressive gallery of motorbikes, Czech and foreign, and a wonderful collection of old planes, trains and automobiles from Czechoslovakia's industrial heyday between the wars when the country's Škoda cars and Tatra soft-top stretch limos were really something to brag about. Other displays trace the development of early photography, while there's an excellent exhibit focusing on Czech architectural feats from the second half of the nineteenth century to the present, and a collection of some of Johannes Kepler and Tycho Brahe's astronomical instruments.

VELETRŽNÍ PALACE (TRADE FAIR PALACE)

Dukelských hrdinů 45 ⓦ www.ngprague.cz. Tues–Sun 10am–6pm. 240Kč. MAP P.119. POCKET MAP E3

The **Veletržní Palace** gets nothing like the number of visitors it should. For not only does the building house Prague's best twentieth-century Czech and international art collection, it is also an architectural sight in itself. Built in 1928, the palace is Prague's ultimate functionalist masterpiece, particularly its vast white interior.

The gallery is bewilderingly big, and virtually impossible to view in its entirety in a single visit. Temporary exhibitions are housed on the first and fifth floors, while the permanent collection occupies the other three. The popular **French art collection** includes works by Rodin, Renoir, Van Gogh, Matisse and Picasso, while other notable **international** exhibits include works by Surrealist Miró, a couple of Henry Moore sculptures and a perforated Lucio Fontana canvas, plus a few canvases by Klimt, Kokoschka, Schiele and Munch, whose influence on early twentieth-century Czech art was considerable.

The **Czech art** section starts with Impressionists Preisler and Slavíček, Cubists Čapek, Gutfreund, Filla and Kubišta, and a whole series of works by František Kupka, by far the most important Czech painter of the last century and (possibly) the first artist in the Western world to exhibit abstract paintings. **Socialist Realism** and **performance art** are not neglected either – plan on spending a full day.

At the time of writing, the most talked-about exhibit was Mucha's Slav Epic (Slovanská epopej), a series of twenty oversized canvases painted between 1912 and 1928 following Alfons Mucha's return to his homeland from Paris. Having spent the Communist period in a disused chateau in Moravia, in the early 2000s the city of Prague decided the Slav Epic belonged in the capital and the cycle now hangs in the Veletržní palác as a "temporary exhibition". Where it will go from here, if it ever does, no one knows.

DOX CENTRE FOR CONTEMPORARY ART

Poupětova 1 ⓦ www.dox.cz. Mon, Sat & Sun 10am–6pm, Wed–Fri 11am–7pm. 180Kč. MAP P.119. POCKET MAP G2

Founded by a private initiative with the goal of making Prague a major European centre for contemporary art, Dox presents mostly group exhibitions that aim to push boundaries and introduce new dialogues. Both Czech and international artists are represented, while the organization's educational programmes, debates and talks make it a pivotal part of the local arts scene. The sprawling building is stunning too, featuring a lovely café and good design shop.

VÝSTAVIŠTĚ (EXHIBITION GROUNDS)

Dukelských hrdinů ⓦ www.vystavistepraha.eu. Tues–Fri 2–9pm, Sat & Sun 10am–9pm. 50Kč or free. MAP P.119, POCKET MAP E2

Since the 1891 Prague Exhibition, **Výstaviště** has served as the city's main trade fair arena and funfair. At the centre of the complex is the flamboyant stained-glass and wrought-iron **Průmysl Palace**, scene of Communist Party rubber-stamp congresses. Several modern structures were built for the 1991 Prague Exhibition, including a circular theatre, **Divadlo Spirála**.

The grounds are busiest at the weekend, particularly in summer, when hordes of Prague families descend to munch hot dogs and drink beer. Apart from the annual trade fairs and special exhibitions, there are a few permanent attractions: the city's **Planetárium** (times vary; 50–150Kč; ⓦ www .planetarium.cz), which has static displays and shows films; the **Maroldovo panorama** (April–Oct Tues–Fri 1–5pm, Sat & Sun 9.30am–5pm; 25Kč), a giant diorama of the 1434 Battle of Lipany; and **Mořský svět** (Mon–Fri 8.30am–6pm, Sat & Sun 9am–7pm; 280Kč; ⓦ www .morsky-svet.cz), an aquarium full of colourful tropical fish, a

few rays and some sea turtles. In the long summer evenings, the *Pražon* restaurant shows outdoor films and hosts concerts, and there are hourly evening performances (230Kč) by the dancing **Křižík Fountain**, devised for the 1891 Exhibition by the Czech inventor František Křižík. Call ☎ 220 103 224 or visit ⓦ krizikovafontana.cz for details.

LAPIDÁRIUM

U Výstaviště ⓦ www.nm.cz. Wed 10am–4pm, Thurs–Sun noon–6pm. 50Kč. MAP P.119, POCKET MAP E2

Official depository for the city's sculptures which are under threat either from demolition or from the weather, the **Lapidárium** houses a much overlooked collection, ranging from the eleventh to the nineteenth century. Some of the statues saved from the perils of Prague's polluted atmosphere, such as the bronze equestrian statue of St George, will be familiar if you've visited Prague Castle; others, such as the figures from the towers of Charles Bridge, are more difficult to inspect closely in their original sites. Many of the original statues from the bridge can be seen here, as well as the ones that were fished out of the

PRŮMYSL PALACE, VÝSTAVIŠTĚ

Getting to Troja and the zoo

To reach Troja and the zoo you can either **walk** from Výstaviště, catch **bus** #112, which runs frequently from metro Nádraží Holešovice, or take a **boat** (April & Sept Sat & Sun only; May–Aug daily; 150Kč; ⓦ www.paroplavba.cz) from the PPS landing place on Rašínovo nábřeží, metro Karlovo náměstí.

Vltava after the flood of 1890.

One outstanding sight is what remains of the **Krocín fountain**, a highly ornate Renaissance work in red marble, which used to grace Staroměstské náměstí (see p.66). Several pompous imperial monuments that were bundled into storage after the demise of the Habsburgs in 1918 round off the museum's collection. By far the most impressive is the bronze statue of Marshal Radecký, scourge of the 1848 revolution, carried aloft on a shield by eight Habsburg soldiers.

STROMOVKA

MAP P.119, POCKET MAP D2

Originally laid out as hunting grounds for the noble occupants of the Castle, **Stromovka** is now Prague's largest and leafiest public park. If you're heading north for Troja and the city zoo, a stroll through the park is by far the most pleasant approach. If you want to explore a little more of the park, head west, sticking to the park's southern border, and you'll eventually come to a neo-Gothic former royal hunting chateau, which served as the seat of the Governor of Bohemia until 1918.

TROJA CHATEAU (TROJSKÝ ZÁMEK)

U trojského zámku 1 ⓦ www.ghmp.cz. April–Oct Tues–Thurs, Sat & Sun 10am–6pm. Fri 1–6pm. 120Kč. MAP P.119. POCKET MAP C1

The **Troja** chateau was designed by Jean-Baptiste Mathey for the powerful Šternberg family towards the end of the seventeenth century. The best features of the rusty-red Baroque facade are the monumental balustrades, where blackened figures of giants and titans battle it out. The star exhibits of the interior are the gushing frescoes depicting the victories of the Habsburg Emperor Leopold I (who reigned from 1657 to 1705) over the Turks, which cover every inch of the walls and ceilings of the grand hall. You also get to wander through the chateau's pristine, trend-setting, French-style formal gardens, the first of their kind in Bohemia.

TROJA CHATEAU

PRAGUE ZOO (ZOOLOGICKÁ ZAHRADA)

U trojského zámku 3 ⊕ www.zoopraha.cz. Daily: March 9am–5pm; April, May, Sept & Oct 9am–6pm; June–Aug 9am–7pm; Nov–Feb 9am–4pm. 200Kč. MAP P.119, POCKET MAP C1

Founded in 1931 on the site of one of Troja's numerous hillside vineyards, Prague's **zoo** has had a lot of money poured into it and now has some very imaginative enclosures. All the usual animals are on show here – including elephants, hippos, giraffes, zebras, big cats and bears – and kids, at least, will enjoy themselves. A bonus in the summer is the **chairlift** (*lanová dráha*) from the duck pond over the enclosures to the top of the hill, where the prize exhibits – a rare breed of miniature horse known as Przewalski – hang out. Other highlights include the red pandas, the giant tortoises, the Komodo dragons, and the bats that actually fly past your face in the Twilight Zone.

BOTANIC GARDENS (BOTANICKÁ ZAHRADA)

Nádvorní 134 ⊕ www.botanicka.cz. Daily: March & Oct 9am–5pm; April–Sept 9am–6pm; Nov–Feb 9am–4pm. 150Kč. POCKET MAP C1

Another reason for coming out to Troja is to visit the city's **botanic gardens**, hidden in the woods to the north of the chateau. The botanic gardens feature a vineyard, a Japanese garden, several glasshouses and great views over Prague. Hidden in the woods a little higher up the hill, there's also a spectacular, curvaceous greenhouse, **Fata Morgana** (same hours but closed Mon), with butterflies flitting about amid the desert and tropical plants.

PRAGUE ZOO

Café

ERHARTOVA CUKRÁRNA

Milady Horákové 56 ⓦwww.erhartovacukrarna
.cz. Daily 10am–7pm. MAP P.119, POCKET MAP E3
First Republic sweet shop with
delectable cakes and typically a
long queue. The café's
functionalist architecture is a
treat for the eyes as well.

Restaurants

HANAVSKÝ PAVILÓN

Letenské sady 173 ☎233 323 641. Daily
11am–midnight. MAP P.119, POCKET MAP E10
Highly ornate wrought-iron
Art Nouveau pleasure pavilion
high above the Vltava, with
stunning views from the
terrace; Czech and international mains 350–500Kč.

LA CRÊPERIE

Janovského 4 ☎220 878 040. Daily
9am–11pm. MAP P.119, POCKET MAP F3
Small and inexpensive
French-run crêperie (with a
kids' play area) serving
buckwheat *galette* and sweet
and savoury pancakes (for
around 120Kč), washed down
with Breton cider.

SVATÁ KLARA (SAINT CLARE)

U trojského zámku 35 ☎233 540 173. Tues–
Sat 6pm–1am. MAP P.119, POCKET MAP C1
Formal restaurant, first opened
in 1679, in a romantic wine
cave setting near the zoo.
Specializes in fondues and
game dishes from 600Kč.

Pubs

FRAKTAL

Šmeralova 1. Daily 11am–midnight. MAP P.119,
POCKET MAP D3
Very popular cellar bar with ad
hoc funky furnishings,

exhibitions and occasional live
music, plus a beer garden and
kids' play area outside.

LETENSKÝ ZÁMEČEK

Letenské sady. Daily 11am–11.30pm.
MAP P.119, POCKET MAP E4
The beer garden, with its great
views down the Vltava, is
cheap and popular with the
locals (the restaurant has gone
upmarket and is less special).

U HOUBAŘE (THE MUSHROOM PICKER)

Dukelských hrdinů 30. Daily 11am–midnight.
MAP P.119, POCKET MAP E3
Comfortable local pub, directly
opposite the Veletržní Palace,
serving Pilsner Urquell and
inexpensive Czech pub food.

Clubs

CROSS CLUB

Plynární 23 ⓦwww.crossclub.cz. Daily
6pm–2am or later. MAP P.119, POCKET MAP F2
Ad hoc labyrinthine club on
several floors, decked out in
arty industrial decor, near
Nádraží Holešovice. The DJs on
each floor range from techno to
ambient. Entry free–120Kč.

MECCA

U Průhonu 3 ⓦwww.mecca.cz. Fri & Sat from
10pm. MAP P.119, POCKET MAP G2
Despite being out in the
grid-plan streets of Prague 7,
this coolly converted factory is
one of the most impressive and
popular clubs in Prague. Entry
100Kč and upwards.

SASAZU

Bubenské nábřeží 306 ☎284 097 444,
ⓦwww.sasazu.cz. MAP P.119, POCKET MAP G3
Prague's biggest venue is
housed in Holešovice's vast
market complex and includes a
club, a major venue for live
gigs and a pan-Asian
restaurant.

ACCOMMODATION

Accommodation

Compared to the price of beer, accommodation in Prague is very expensive. If you're looking for a double and can pay around 4000Kč (€150) a night then you'll find plenty of choice. At the other end of the scale, there are numerous hostels charging around 400Kč (€15) for a bed. However, there's a shortage of decent, inexpensive to middle-range places. You can, however, get some very good deals – and undercut the often exorbitant rack rates – by booking online well in advance. Given that Prague can be pretty busy all year round, it's not a bad idea to book ahead in any case. All accommodation prices in this chapter are for the cheapest double room in high season; breakfast is usually included in the price, unless otherwise stated.

Hradčany

DOMUS HENRICI > Loretánská 11, tram #22 to Pohořelec ☎ 220 511 369, Ⓦ www.domus-henrici.cz. MAP P.40, POCKET MAP B11. Stylish, discreet hotel in a fabulous location, with just eight rooms/apartments, some with splendid views. Run in conjunction with *Domus Balthasar* on Mostecká, by Charles Bridge. **3570Kč**

QUESTENBERK > Úvoz 15, tram #22 from Ⓜ Malostranská to Pohořelec ☎ 220 407 600, Ⓦ www.questenberk .cz. MAP P.40, POCKET MAP A12. From the outside, this hotel looks like a Baroque chapel, but inside it's been totally modernized. Rooms are smart but plain, though the views from some are superb. **3130Kč**

SAVOY PRAGUE > Keplerova 6, tram #22 from Ⓜ Malostranská to Pohořelec ☎ 224 302 430, Ⓦ www .hotelsavoyprague.com. MAP P.40, POCKET MAP A5. Dated, charming luxury hotel on Hradčany's western edge, still sporting its original Art Nouveau facade. Popular for its marble bathrooms and free minibar, there's also a lovely lounge area. Breakfast extra. **3300Kč**

U KRÁLE KARLA (KING CHARLES) > Úvoz 4, tram #22 to Pohořelec ☎ 257 531 211, Ⓦ www.ukralekarla.cz. MAP P.40, POCKET MAP B11. Possibly the most tastefully exquisite of all the small luxury hotels in the castle district, with beautiful antique furnishings and stained-glass windows. Situated at the top of Nerudova, it's a steep walk from the nearest tram stop, however. **3300Kč**

U RAKA (THE CRAYFISH) > Černínská 10, tram #22 from Ⓜ Malostranská to Brusnice ☎ 220 511 100, Ⓦ www.hoteluraka.cz. MAP P.40, POCKET MAP A10. The perfect hideaway, six double rooms in a little half-timbered, eighteenth-century cottage in Nový Svět. No children under 12 or dogs, and advance reservation a must. **2430Kč**

U ZLATÉHO KONÍČKA (GOLDEN HORSE) > Úvoz 8, tram #22 to Pohořelec ☎ 603 841 790, Ⓦ www .goldenhorse.cz. MAP P.40, POCKET MAP B11. Small, plain, clean, en-suite rooms at real bargain prices in a perfect location on the way up to the Hrad. Breakfast is served in the brick-vaulted cellar. **1600Kč**

Malá Strana

ALCHYMIST GRAND HOTEL > Tržiště 19, tram #12, #20 or #22 to Malostranské náměstí ☎ 257 286 011, Ⓦ www.alchymisthotel.com. MAP P.48–49, POCKET MAP C12. Total decadent luxury abounds in this sixteenth-century palace, which has been tastefully converted into a secluded spa hotel, complete with Indonesian masseuses and an indoor pool. **8000Kč**

ARIA > Tržiště 9, tram #12, #20 or #22 to Malostranské náměstí ☎ 225 334 111, Ⓦ www.ariahotel.net. MAP P.48–49, POCKET MAP C12. A popular hotel with musically themed rooms and a special music library. Guests can enjoy the stunning roof terrace and private access to one of Prague Castle's gardens. **5500Kč**

DIENTZENHOFER > Nosticova 2, tram #12, #20 or #22 to Hellichova ☎ 257 311 319, Ⓦ www.dientzenhofer.cz. MAP P.48–49, POCKET MAP D12. Birthplace of the eponymous architect Kilian Ignác Dientzenhofer and a very popular and unpretentious pension, as it's one of the few reasonably priced places (anywhere in Prague) to have wheelchair access. **2700Kč**

DŮM U VELKÉ BOTY (THE BIG SHOE) > Vlašská 30, tram #12, #20 or #22 to Malostranské náměstí ☎ 257 532 088, Ⓦ www.dumuvelkeboty.cz. MAP P.48–49, POCKET MAP B12. The sheer discreetness of this pension, in a lovely old building in the quiet backstreets, is one of its main draws. Run by a very friendly couple, who speak good English, it has a series of cosy rooms, replete with genuine antiques, some en suite, some not. Breakfast is extra, but worth it. **3300Kč**

LITTLE TOWN BUDGET HOTEL > Malostranské náměstí 11, tram #12, #20 or #22 to Malostranské náměstí ☎ 242 406 964, Ⓦ www.littletown hotel.cz. MAP P.48–49, POCKET MAP C12. Possibly Malá Strana's cheapest digs, with basic private rooms sleeping up to four people. It has its own kitchen, which you share with the hostel rooms in the same building. **1600Kč**

LOKAL INN > Míšenská 12, tram #12, #20 or #22 to Malostranské náměstí ☎ 257 014 800, Ⓦ www .lokalinn.cz. MAP P.48–49, POCKET MAP D12. Top-drawer boutique hotel where the original features of the Baroque building have been preserved to provide a backdrop for the interesting design features. There is also a superb contemporary restaurant downstairs. **3300Kč**

LUNDBORG > U Lužického semináře 3, tram #12, #20 or #22 to Malostranské náměstí ☎ 257 011 911, Ⓦ www .lundborg.se. MAP P.48–49, POCKET MAP D12. Very stylish Swedish-run apartment suites with Baroque painted ceilings and tasteful furnishings, as well as jacuzzis and free internet access in every room. Situated in the thick of it, right by the Charles Bridge tower. **Suites from 5000Kč**

NERUDA > Nerudova 44, tram #12, #20 or #22 to Malostranské náměstí ☎ 257 535 557, Ⓦ www.designhotel neruda.com. MAP P.48–49, POCKET MAP B11. This stylish hotel is a fair walk up Nerudova, but it has a funky, glass-roofed foyer, uses lots of cool natural stone, and boasts smart, minimalist modern decor in the rooms. **3600Kč**

NOSTICOVA > Nosticova 1, tram #12, #20 or #22 to Hellichova ☎ 257 312 513, Ⓦ www.nosticova.com. MAP P.48–49, POCKET MAP D12. Baroque house with ten beautifully restored rooms replete with antique furnishings, sumptuous bathrooms and some with kitchens, on a tranquil square not far from Charles Bridge. **5400Kč**

SAX > Jánský vršek 3, tram #12, #20 or #22 to Malostranské náměstí ☎ 257 531 268, Ⓦ www.hotelsax .cz. MAP P.48–49, POCKET MAP C12. Perfectly located in the backstreets off Nerudova, this hotel has gone for a remarkably convincing groovy retro 1960s look, but it's also a very well-run, well-equipped place with a DVD library. **3300Kč**

U KARLOVA MOSTU > Na Kampě 15, tram #12, #20 or #22 to Malostranské náměstí ☎ 234 652 808, Ⓦ www .archibald.cz. MAP P.48–49, POCKET MAP E12. Situated on a lovely tree-lined square, just off Charles Bridge, the rooms in this former brewery (now a pub-restaurant) have real character, despite the modern fittings. **3300Kč**

U PÁVA (THE PEACOCK) > U lužického semináře 32 Ⓜ Malostranská ☎ 257 533 573, Ⓦ www.hotel-upava.cz. MAP P.48–49, POCKET MAP E11. Tucked away in the quiet backstreets, *U páva* boasts some sumptuously over-the-top Baroque fittings – real and repro. Some rooms have views over to the castle, and service is good. **3400Kč**

U ZLATÉ STUDNĚ (THE GOLDEN WELL) > U zlaté studně 4, tram #12, #20 or #22 to Malostranské náměstí ☎ 257 011 213, Ⓦ www.goldenwell .cz. MAP P.48–49, POCKET MAP D11. A special location: tucked into the terraces below Prague Castle, next to the terraced gardens, with incredible views across the rooftops. The rooms feature lots of original ceilings, and there's a good restaurant with a wonderful summer terrace. **7000Kč**

U ZLATÝCH NŮŽEK (THE GOLDEN SCISSORS) > Na Kampě 6, tram #12, #20 or #22 to Malostranské náměstí ☎ 257 530 473, Ⓦ www.uzlatychnuzek .cz. MAP P.48–49, POCKET MAP E12. Ten rooms with parquet flooring, the odd beam and simple modern furnishings. On Kampa island, close to Charles Bridge. **3500Kč**

Staré Město

ARCADIA OLD TOWN > Kožná 6 and 13 Ⓜ Můstek ☎ 724 027 525, Ⓦ www .arcadiaoldtown.com. MAP P.62–63, POCKET MAP G12. Cosy apartments right in the heart of the labyrinth of streets south of Old Town Square. Decor is bright, cheerful and modern. **Apartments from 3500Kč**

ČERNÝ SLON (BLACK ELEPHANT) > Týnská 1 Ⓜ Náměstí Republiky ☎ 222 321 521, Ⓦ www.hotel cernyslon.cz. MAP P.62–63, POCKET MAP G11. Another ancient building tucked away off Old Town Square by the north portal of the Týn church, now tastefully converted into a very comfortable small hotel. **3000Kč**

CLOISTER INN Konviktská 14 Ⓜ Národní třída ☎ 224 211 020, Ⓦ www.hotel-cloister.com. MAP P.62–63, POCKET MAP F13. Pleasant, well-equipped hotel housed in a nunnery in one of the backstreets; the rooms are simply furnished with modern fittings, and the location is good. **2400Kč**

GRAND HOTEL BOHEMIA > Kralodvorská 4 Ⓜ Náměstí Republiky ☎ 234 608 111, Ⓦ www.grand hotelbohemia.cz. MAP.62–63, POCKET MAP H12. Probably the most elegant luxury hotel in the Old Town, just behind the Obecní dům, with some very tasty Art Nouveau decor and all the amenities you'd expect from an Austrian outfit. **6000Kč**

GRAND HOTEL PRAHA > Staroměstské náměstí 22 Ⓜ Můstek ☎ 221 632 556, Ⓦ www.grand hotelpraha.cz. MAP P.62–63, POCKET MAP G12. If you want a room overlooking the astronomical clock on Old Town Square, then book in here, well in advance. There are beautiful antique furnishings, big oak ceilings, but only a very few rooms, including a single, as well an attic suite for four. **4300Kč**

HOSTEL PRAGUE TÝN > Týnská 21 Ⓜ Náměstí Republiky ☎ 224 808 301, Ⓦ www.tyn.prague-hostels.cz. MAP P.62–63, POCKET MAP H11. Prague's most centrally located hostel is a basic affair with shared facilities and no breakfast. It's located in a quiet courtyard (with a veggie Indian café in it) a stone's throw from Old Town Square. **Doubles from 1300Kč; five-bed dorms 490Kč**

JOSEF > Rybná 20 Ⓜ Náměstí Republiky ☎ 221 700 901, Ⓦ www .hoteljosef.com. MAP P.62–63, POCKET MAP H11. Staré Město's top designer hotel exudes modern professionalism, the lobby is a symphony in off-white efficiency and the rooms continue the crisply maintained minimalist theme. **3800Kč**

LIPPERT HOTEL > Mikulášská 2
Ⓜ Staroměstská ☎ 224 232 250,
Ⓦ www.hotel-lippert.cz. MAP P.62–63,
POCKET MAP G12. So central it's
ridiculous, yet with friendly and
helpful staff; well-appointed rooms,
hand-painted ceilings and some with
incredible views onto Old Town Square,
and quieter ones at the back. **4000Kč**

PACHTŮV PALACE > Karoliny Světlé
34 Ⓜ Národní třída ☎ 234 705 111,
Ⓦ www.pachtuvpalace.com. MAP
P.62–63, POCKET MAP F12. Former Baroque
palace, now luxury hotel, in the heart of
the Old Town, with charming and efficient
staff, rooms and suites decked in a blend of
antique and repro furniture. **7500Kč**

RESIDENCE ŘETĚZOVÁ > Řetězová
9 Ⓜ Staroměstská ☎ 222 221 800,
Ⓦ www.retezova.com. MAP P.62–63,
POCKET MAP F12. Attractive apartments
of all sizes, with kitchenettes, wooden or
stone floors, Gothic vaulting or wooden
beams and repro furnishings throughout.
Apartments from 5000Kč

RITCHIE'S HOSTEL > Karlova 9 and
13 Ⓜ Staroměstská ☎ 222 221 229,
Ⓦ www.ritchieshostel.cz. MAP P.62–63,
POCKET MAP F12. In the midst of the
human river that is Karlova, this Old Town
hostel is clean, with accommodation
ranging from en-suite doubles to
twelve-bed dorms; no in-house laundry
or cooking facilities. **Dorm beds 405Kč,
doubles from 1860Kč**

SAVIC > Jilská 7 Ⓜ Národní třída
☎ 224 248 555, Ⓦ www.savic.eu.
MAP P.62–63, POCKET MAP G12. This
hotel, in the heart of the Old Town,
has retained plenty of period features:
painted ceilings, vaulting, exposed
beams and the like. Staff are as helpful
as can be, and the buffet breakfast is
superb. **6500Kč**

TRAVELLERS HOSTEL > Dlouhá 33
Ⓜ Náměstí Republiky ☎ 777 738 608,
Ⓦ www.travellers.cz. MAP P.62–63,
POCKET MAP H11. Very central party
hostel (although it's not the cleanest of
places), situated above the *Roxy* nightclub.
Breakfast is included. **Dorm beds from
390Kč, doubles from 1600Kč**

U MEDVÍDKŮ (THE LITTLE BEARS) >
Na Perštýně 7 Ⓜ Národní třída ☎ 224
211 916, Ⓦ www.umedvidku.cz. MAP
P.62–63, POCKET MAP G13. The rooms
above this famous Prague pub are plainly
furnished, quiet considering the locale,
and therefore something of an Old Town
bargain; booking ahead essential. **2200Kč**

UNITAS HOUSE > Bartolomějská
9 Ⓜ Národní třída ☎ 224 230 533,
Ⓦ www.unitas.cz. MAP P.62–63,
POCKET MAP F13. Set in a Franciscan
nunnery, *Unitas House* has big, tastefully
furnished bedrooms with comfy beds,
while its bathrooms are of similarly
generous proportions. **3500Kč**

U TŘÍ BUBNŮ (THE THREE DRUMS)
> U radnice 8–10 Ⓜ Staroměstská
☎ 224 214 855, Ⓦ www.utribubnu
.cz. MAP P.62–63, POCKET MAP G12.
Small hotel just off Old Town Square with
five tastefully furnished rooms, either
with original fifteenth-century wooden
ceilings or lots of exposed beams. No lift
but plenty of stairs. **4300Kč**

Wenceslas Square and northern Nové Město

ALCRON > Štěpánská 40 Ⓜ Můstek or
Muzeum ☎ 222 820 000, Ⓦ www
.radissonblu.com. MAP P.88, POCKET
MAP H14. Giant 1930s luxury hotel, just
off Wenceslas Square, superbly restored to
its former Art Deco glory by the Radisson
chain. Double rooms here are without doubt
the most luxurious and tasteful you'll find
in Nové Město. **3500Kč**

Our Picks

Budget choice: *Czech Inn* p.133
Central hotel: *Grand Hotel Praha*
   p.130
Boutique: *Lokal Inn* p.129
Room with a view: *U zlaté studně*
   p.130
Romance: *Domus Henrici* p.128
Luxury: *Paříž* p.132

HARMONY > Na Poříčí 31 Ⓜ Florenc ☎ 272 114 444 Ⓦ www.hotelharmony .cz. MAP P.88, POCKET MAP K11. For those on a budget, this is a very sound low-cost option a dumpling's throw from the main sights. Good for those who want to sleep, shower, surf the net and breakfast – for medieval grandeur go elsewhere. **2000Kč**

HOSTEL ROSEMARY > Růžová 5 Ⓜ Můstek or Hlavní nádraží ☎ 222 211 124, Ⓦ www.praguecityhostel .cz. MAP P.88, POCKET MAP J13. Clean, modern hostel a short walk from the main train station, Praha hlavní nádraží. Three- to twelve-bed mixed dorms, plus doubles with or without en-suite and kitchen facilities. Communal kitchen and free internet, but breakfast not included. **Dorms from 320Kč, doubles from 1700Kč**

IMPERIAL > Na poříčí 15 Ⓜ Náměstí Republiky ☎ 246 011 600, Ⓦ www .hotel-imperial.cz. MAP P.88, POCKET MAP J11. Despite describing itself as Art Deco, this place is actually more of an Art Nouveau masterpiece. Built in 1914, the public rooms are simply dripping with period ceramic friezes; the rest of the hotel is standard twenty-first-century luxury. **6300Kč**

PALACE > Panská 12 Ⓜ Můstek ☎ 224 093 111, Ⓦ www.palacehotel .cz. MAP P.88, POCKET MAP H13. Luxury five-star hotel just off Wenceslas Square, renowned for its excellent service and facilities – rooms are spotless and the buffet breakfast is top-class. **4100Kč**

PAŘÍŽ > U Obecního domu 1 Ⓜ Náměstí Republiky ☎ 222 195 195, Ⓦ www.hotel-paris.cz. MAP P.88, POCKET MAP H11. This is a good top-notch hotel with plenty of *fin de siècle* atmosphere still intact – it was used as the setting for Bohumil Hrabal's *I Served the King of England*. **6000Kč**

SALVATOR > Truhlářská 10 Ⓜ Náměstí Republiky ☎ 222 312 234, Ⓦ www.salvator.cz. MAP P.88, POCKET MAP J11. This is a very good location for the price, just a minute's walk from náměstí Republiky, with small but

clean rooms (the cheaper ones with shared facilities), and all set around a courtyard. The buffet breakfast is good, and the staff are friendly. **3500Kč**

Národní and southern Nové Město

HOSTEL EMMA > Na Zderaze 10 Ⓜ Karlovo náměstí ☎ 222 521 269, Ⓦ www.hostel-emma.com. MAP P.97, POCKET MAP F15. Centrally located hostel for those with public transport phobias. Free linens and internet make the spartan rooms a bit more tolerable, and the bathrooms are in good condition. **Dorm beds from 300Kč**

HOTEL 16 – U SV KATEŘINY > Kateřinská 16, tram #18 or #24 ☎ 224 920 636, Ⓦ www.hotel16.cz. MAP P.97, POCKET MAP E7. Really friendly, family-run hotel offering small, plain but clean en-suite rooms. There's a small terraced garden at the back and botanic gardens nearby. **3500Kč**

HOTEL JUNGMANN > Jungmannovo náměstí 2 Ⓜ Můstek ☎ 224 219 501, Ⓦ www.antikhotels.com. MAP P.97, POCKET MAP G13. Small hotel in a very tall (no lift), narrow building just a step away from the bottom of Wenceslas Square. Rooms are spacious – especially the suites – and decked out in tasteful modern furnishings. **3200Kč**

ICON HOTEL > V jámě 6 Ⓜ Můstek ☎ 221 634 100, Ⓦ www.iconhotel.eu. MAP P.97, POCKET MAP H14. Modern designer hotel, whose white-walled rooms are equipped with large, handmade Hästens beds. All-day à la carte breakfast will suit late risers. **2700Kč**

MÁNES > Myslíkova 20 Ⓜ Karlovo náměstí ☎ 221 516 388, Ⓦ www .hotelmanes.cz. MAP P.97, POCKET MAP F15. Star ratings mean little in the Czech Republic, but the *Mánes*, named after the nineteenth-century Czech artist, deserves every one of its four twinklers. The fifty rooms are finished with contemporary panache, the bathrooms are spacious and stylish, and the location near Karlovo náměstí puts you near enough to the main sights. 2700Kč

MISS SOPHIE'S > Melounová 3 Ⓜ I. P. Pavlova ☎ 246 032 620, Ⓦ www.miss-sophies.com. MAP P.97, POCKET MAP E7. Beautiful and friendly designer hostel close to the cool Vinohrady district. Everything from dorm rooms to apartments are available. **Dorm beds from 520Kč, doubles from 2100Kč**

Vyšehrad, Vinohrady and Žižkov

ANNA > Budečská 17 Ⓜ Náměstí Míru ☎ 222 513 111, Ⓦ www .hotelanna.cz. MAP P.109, POCKET MAP F7. Plain but smartly appointed rooms, warm friendly staff and a decent location make this a popular choice in Vinohrady, with trams and the metro close by. 1600Kč

CLOWN AND BARD > Bořivojova 102, tram #5, #9 or #26 to Husinecká ☎ 222 716 453, Ⓦ www.clownandbard .com. MAP P.109, POCKET MAP G6. Žižkov hostel that attracts backpackers who like to party. Still, it's clean, undeniably cheap, stages events and has laundry facilities. Veggie breakfast extra. **Dorm beds from 300Kč, doubles from 1200Kč**

CZECH INN > Francouzská 76, tram #4, #22 ☎ 267 267 600, Ⓦ www.czech-inn.com. MAP P.109, POCKET MAP G8. Upbeat, designer hostel that feels and looks like a hotel, with friendly and helpful staff and a choice of dormitories and private rooms. **Dorm beds from 540Kč, doubles from 2000Kč**

DAHLIA INN > Lípová 1444/20, tram #22 to Štěpánská ☎ 222 517 518, Ⓦ www.dahliainn.com. MAP P.109, POCKET MAP E7. Modern and colourful, *Dahlia* will delight you with its contemporary rooms, superb service and convenient location between Wenceslas Square and the Vinohrady neighbourhood. With only eight rooms, advance booking is advised. 2700Kč

EHRLICH > Koněvova 79, Žižkov, tram #9, #10, #11 or #16 to Biskupcova ☎ 236 040 555, Ⓦ www.hotelehrlich.cz. MAP P.109, POCKET MAP H5. Few tourists would actually choose to stay in Žižkov, but perhaps if they saw this spacious, well-maintained hotel on the district's main thoroughfare they might consider it as an option. Some rooms have baths and air conditioning and there's a decent café in the building. 1600Kč

GALILEO > Bruselská 3, tram #6 or #11 to Bruselská ☎ 222 500 129, Ⓦ www.hotelgalileoprague.com. MAP P.109, POCKET MAP F7. Chic, modern hotel furnished with style, offering apartments as well as en-suite doubles. 3800Kč

Arrival

Prague is one of Europe's smaller capital cities. The airport lies just over 10km northwest of the city centre, with only a bus link or taxi to get you into town. Both the international train stations and the main bus terminal are linked to the centre by the fast and efficient metro system.

By plane

Prague's **Václav Havel airport** (☎ 220 111 888, ⓦ www.prg.aero) is connected to the city by minibus, bus and taxi. The Cedaz (ⓦ www .cedaz.cz) shared **minibus** service (daily 7.30am–7pm; every 30min) takes you to V celnici, off náměstí Republiky (journey time 30min); the journey currently costs 150Kč. Another option is the **Prague Airport Shuttle** (ⓦ www .prague-airport-shuttle.com), which will take you into town for 500Kč for up to four passengers.

The cheapest way to get into town is on local **bus #119** (daily 5am–midnight; every 15–20min; journey time 25min), which stops frequently and ends its journey outside Dejvická metro station. You can buy your ticket from the public transport (DP) information desk in arrivals (daily 7am–10pm), or from the nearby machines or newsagents. If you're going to use public transport while in Prague, you might as well buy a pass straight away (see opposite). If you arrive between midnight and 5am, you can catch the hourly **night bus**
#510 to Divoká Šárka, the terminus for night tram #51, which will take you on to Národní in the centre of town. Another cheap alternative is **Linka AE** (Airport Express), which connects to Dejvická metro (60Kč) and Praha hlavní nádraží (daily 5.45am–10.05pm; every 30min; 60Kč).

If you're thinking of taking a **taxi** from the airport into the centre, AAA Taxi (☎ 14014, ⓦ www.aaataxi .cz) is the reputable agency running from the airport. They have a rank outside arrivals and the journey to the city centre should cost around 500–600Kč.

By train

International trains arrive either at Praha hlavní nádraží, on the edge of Nové Město and Vinohrady, or at Praha-Holešovice, which lies north of the city centre. At both stations you'll find exchange outlets, 24hr left-luggage offices (úschovna zavazadel) and accommodation agencies (plus a tourist office at Hlavní nádraží). Both stations are on metro lines, and Hlavní nádraží is only a five-minute walk from Václavské náměstí (Wenceslas Square).

By bus

Prague's **main bus terminal** is Praha-Florenc (ⓜFlorenc), on the eastern edge of Nové Město, where virtually all long-distance international and domestic services terminate. There's a tourist office here, as well as a left-luggage office and a computer for checking bus times.

Getting around

The centre of Prague is reasonably small and best explored on foot. At some point, however, particularly to reach some of the more widely dispersed attractions, you'll need to use the city's cheap and efficient public transport system (*dopravní podnik* or *DP*; ⊕ www.dpp.cz), which comprises the metro and a network of trams and buses. You can get free maps, tickets and passes from the DP **information offices** (☏ 296 191 817) at both airport terminals (daily 7am–9pm), from Holešovice train station (Mon–Fri 7am–9pm), Můstek metro (Mon–Fri 7am–6pm), Muzeum metro (daily 7am–9pm) and Anděl metro (Mon–Fri 7am–9pm).

Tickets and passes

Most Praguers buy annual passes, and to avoid having to understand the complexities of the single ticket system, you too are best off buying a **travel pass** (*jízdenka*) for either 24 hours (*1 den*; 110Kč) or three days (*3 dny*; 310Kč); no photos or ID are needed, though you must punch it to validate when you first use it. All the passes are available from DP outlets and ticket machines.

Despite the multitude of buttons on the **ticket machines** – found inside all metro stations and at some bus and tram stops – there are just two basic choices. The 24Kč version (*krátkodobá*) allows you to travel for 30 minutes on the trams or buses, or up to five stops on the metro; it's also known as a *nepřestupní jízdenka*, or "no change ticket", although you can in fact change metro lines (but not buses or trams). The 32Kč version (*základní*) is valid for 90 minutes, during which you may change trams, buses or metro lines as many times as you like, hence its name, *přestupní*

jízdenka, or "changing ticket". A full-price ticket is called *plnocenná*; discounted tickets (*zvýhodněna*) are available for children aged 6–15; under-6s travel free.

To buy a ticket from one of the machines, press the appropriate button followed by the *výdej*/enter button, then put your money in. The machines do give change, but if you don't have enough coins, the person on duty in the metro office by the barriers can give you change or sell you a ticket. Tickets can also be bought from a tobacconist (*tabák*), street kiosk, newsagent, PIS office or any place that displays the yellow DP sticker. When you enter the metro, or board a tram or bus, you must validate your ticket in one of the machines to hand.

There are no barriers, but plain-clothes inspectors (*revizoři*) make random checks and will issue an on-the-spot fine of 800Kč to anyone caught without a valid ticket or pass; controllers should show you their ID (a small metal disc) and give you a receipt (*paragon*).

Metro

Prague's futuristic, Soviet-built **metro** is fast, smooth and ultra-clean, running daily 5am till midnight with trains every two minutes during peak hours, slowing down to every four to ten minutes by late evening. Its three lines intersect at various points in the city centre.

The stations are fairly discreetly marked above ground with the metro logo, in green (line A), yellow (line B) or red (line C). Inside the metro, *výstup* means exit and *přestup* will lead you to one of the connecting lines. The digital clock at the end of the platform tells you what time it is and how long it was since the last train.

Trams

The electric tram (*tramvaj*) system negotiates Prague's hills and cobbles with remarkable dexterity. Modern rolling stock is gradually being introduced, but most of Prague's trams (traditionally red and cream) date back to the Communist era. After the metro, trams are the fastest and most efficient way of getting around, running every 6–8min at peak times, and every 5–15min at other times – check the timetables posted at every stop (*zastávka*), which list the departure times from that stop. Note that it is the custom for younger folk to vacate their seat when an older person enters the carriage.

Tram #22, which runs from Vinohrady to Hradčany via the centre of town and Malá Strana, is a good, cheap way of sightseeing, though you should beware of pickpockets. At weekends from March to November, nostalgic tram #91 runs from the Transport Museum to Výstaviště, via Prague Castle, Malá Strana, Wenceslas Square and náměstí Republiky and back again (Sat & Sun hourly noon–5.30pm; 40min; 35Kč). **Night trams** (*noční tramvaje*; #51–58; every 30–40min; roughly midnight–4.30am) run on different routes from the daytime ones, though at some point all night trams pass along Lazarská in Nové Město.

Buses

You'll rarely need to get on a **bus** (*autobus*) in Prague, since most of them keep well out of the centre. If you're intent upon visiting the zoo, staying in one of the city's more obscure suburbs, or taking the cheap option to the airport, you will need to use them: their hours of operation

are similar to those of the trams (though generally less frequent). **Night buses** (*noční autobusy*) run once an hour midnight–5am.

Ferries and boats

The public transport system runs a handful of small summer **ferry services** (*přívoz*) on the Vltava between the islands and the riverbanks (April–Oct daily 6am–10pm, every 30min). In the summer months there are also regular boat trips on the River Vltava run by the PPS (Pražská paroplavební společnost; ☎ 224 930 017, ⓦ www.paroplavba .cz) from just south of Jiráskův most on Rašínovo nábřeží. Three boats a day in summer run to Troja (see p.123) in the northern suburbs (May to Aug daily; April & Sept Sat and Sun only; 160Kč one-way).

The PPS also offers boat trips around Prague (May–Sept daily 1–2hr; 220–290Kč) on board a 1930s paddlesteamer.

Taxis

Taxis are, theoretically at least, relatively cheap. However, many Prague taxi drivers will attempt to overcharge, particularly at taxi ranks close to the tourist sights. Officially, the initial fare on the meter should be around 40Kč plus around 20Kč/km within Prague and 4–6Kč/min waiting time. The best advice is to have your hotel or pension call you one – you then qualify for a cheaper rate – rather than hail one or pick one up at the taxi ranks. The cab company with the best reputation is AAA Taxi (☎ 14014, ⓦ www.aaataxi.cz), which has metered taxis all over Prague.

Directory A–Z

Addresses

The street name is always written before the building number in Prague addresses. The city is divided into numbered postal districts: of the areas covered in the Guide, central Prague is Prague 1; southern Nové Město and half of Vinohrady is Prague 2; the rest of Vinohrady and Žižkov is Prague 3; Holešovice is Prague 7.

Bike rental

City Bike, Královodvorská 5. April–Oct daily 9am–7pm; ☎776 180 284, ⓦwww.citybike-prague.com; ⓜNáměstí Republiky.

Children

Despite a friendly attitude to kids and babies in general, you'll see very few children in museums and galleries, or in pubs, restaurants or cafés. Apart from the zoo and the mirror maze, there aren't very many attractions specifically aimed at kids. The castle and the Petřín funicular usually go down well, as does a ride on a tram.

Cinema

Cinema tickets still cost less than 200Kč. Most films are shown in the original language with subtitles (*titulky* or *české titulky*); some blockbusters are dubbed (*dabing* or *česká verze*). Occasionally you can get to see a Czech film with English subtitles (*anglický titulky*).

Crime

There are two main types of police: the **Policie** are the national force, with white shirts, navy blue jackets and grey trousers, while the **Městská** policie, run by the Prague city authorities, are distinguishable by their all-black uniforms. The main central police station is at Bartolomějská 6, Staré Město.

Cultural institutes

American Center, Tržiště 13 ⓦwww.americkecentrum.cz; **Austrian Cultural Institute**, Jungmannovo náměstí 18 ⓦwww.oekfprag.at; **Instituto Cervantes**, Na rybníčku 6 ⓦpraga.cervantes.es; **Goethe Institut**, Masarykovo nábřeží 32 ⓦwww.goethe.de/prag; **Institut Français**, Štěpánská 35 ⓦwww.ifp.cz; **Instituto Italiano di Cultura**, Šporkova 14 ⓦwww.iicpraga.esteri.it.

Disabilities

The guidebook *Accessible Prague/Přístupná Praha* is available from the Prague Wheelchair Association (Pražská organizace vozíčkářů), Benediktská 6 ☎224 827 210, ⓦwww.pov.cz.

Electricity

The standard continental 220 volts AC. Most European appliances should work as long as you have an adaptor for continental-style two-pin round plugs. North Americans will need this plus a transformer.

Embassies

Australia, Klimentská 10, Nové Město ☎296 578 350; **Canada**, Ve Struhách 2, Bubeneč ☎272 101 800, ⓦwww.canada.cz; **Ireland**, Tržiště 13, Malá Strana ☎257 530 061; **New Zealand**, Václavské náměstí 11 (Wenceslas Square) ☎234 784 777; **UK**, Thunovská 14, Malá Strana ☎257 402 111, ⓦwww.gov.uk/government/world/organisations/british-embassy-prague; **US**, Tržiště 15, Malá Strana ☎257 022 000, ⓦwww.prague.usembassy.gov.

Emergencies

All services ☎112; Ambulance ☎155; Police ☎158; Fire ☎150.

Health

For an English-speaking doctor, go to Nemocnice na Homolce, Roentgenova 2, Motol (☏ 257 271 111). If it's an emergency, dial ☏ 155 for an ambulance. For an emergency dentist, contact Canadian Medical Centre (☏ 724 300 312, ⓦ www .cmcpraha.cz). For a 24hr chemist, try Palackého 5 (☏ 224 946 962) or Belgická 37 (☏ 222 513 396).

Internet

Plenty of Prague's hotels and cafés have free wi-fi.

Left luggage

Prague's main bus and train stations have lockers and/or a 24hr left-luggage office, with instructions in English.

LGBT Prague

There's a friendly and well-established gay and lesbian scene with its spiritual heart in the leafy suburbs of Vinohrady and the more run-down neighbourhood of Žižkov. Up-to-date listings are available from ⓦ www.prague.gayguide.net.

Lost property

The main train stations have lost property offices – look for the sign *ztráty a nálezy* – and there's a central municipal one at Karoliny Světlé 5 (Mon–Fri only). If you've lost your passport, then get in touch with your embassy (see p.139).

Money

The currency is the Czech crown or koruna česká (abbreviated to Kč or CZK). At the time of going to press there were roughly 37Kč to the pound sterling, 27Kč to the euro and around 25Kč to the US dollar. For up-to-date exchange rates, consult ⓦ www .oanda.com or ⓦ www.xe.com. Notes come in 100Kč, 200Kč, 500Kč, 1000Kč and 2000Kč (and less frequently 5000Kč) denominations; coins as 1Kč, 2Kč, 5Kč, 10Kč, 20Kč and 50Kč. Banking hours are Monday–Friday 8am–5pm, often with a break at lunchtime. ATMs can be found across the city.

Newspapers

You can get most foreign dailies and magazines at the kiosks at the bottom of Wenceslas Square, outside metro Můstek.

Opening hours

Shops in Prague are generally open Monday–Friday 9am–5pm, though most tourist shops stay open until 6pm or later. Some shops close by noon or 1pm on Saturday and close all day Sunday, but there's no law against opening on Sundays and many shops in the centre do (including both main supermarkets/department stores). Museums and galleries are generally open Tuesday–Sunday 10am–6pm.

Phones

Most public phones take only phone cards (*telefonní karty*), available from post offices, tobacconists and some shops (prices vary). The best-value ones are pre-paid phone cards that give you a phone number and a code to enter. There are instructions in English, and if you press the appropriate button the language on the digital read-out will change to English. If you have any problems, ring ☏ 1181 to get through to international information. Phone numbers in Prague consist of nine digits. There are no separate city/area codes in the Czech Republic.

Post

The main 24hr post office (*pošta*) is at Jindřišská 14, Nové Město ☏ 840 111 244; take a ticket and wait for your number to come up. A more tourist-friendly branch exists in the third courtyard of Prague Castle.

Prague Card

The Prague Card (ⓦwww.prague card.com) is valid for two, three or four days and gives free entry into over fifty sights for 1280/1540/1780Kč (though not including the sights of the former Ghetto of Josefov). All in all, the card will save you a lot of hassle, but not necessarily that much money. The card is available from all travel information and PIS offices.

Smoking

The Czechs have yet to give in to the EU trend of banning smoking in pubs and restaurants, though all establishments must display a sign on the door stating if they are smoking, non-smoking or both.

Time

The Czech Republic is on Central European Time (CET), one hour ahead of Britain and six hours ahead of EST, with the clocks going forward in spring and back again some time in autumn – the exact date changes from year to year. Generally speaking, Czechs use the 24-hour clock.

Tipping

Tipping is normal practice in cafés, bars, restaurants and taxis, usually done simply by rounding up the total. For example, if the waiter tots up the bill and asks you for 138Kč, you should give him 150Kč and tell him to keep the change. Automatic service charges that appear on the bill are not standard Czech practice.

Toilets

Apart from the automatic ones in central Prague, public toilets (záchody, toalety or WC) are few and far between. In some, you have to buy toilet paper (by the sheet) from the attendant, whom you will also have to pay as you enter. Standards of hygiene can be low. Gentlemen should head for muži or páni; ladies should head for ženy or dámy.

Tourist information

The tourist office is **Prague City Tourism**, whose main branch is within the **Staroměstská radnice** on Staroměstské náměstí (daily 9am–7pm; ⓦwww.praguecitytourism .cz). There are additional offices at **Rytířská 12** (daily 9am–7pm), Staré Město (daily 9am–7pm; ⓜMůstek), in **Wenceslas Square** (daily 10am–6pm), plus an office in the **airport** (daily 9am–7pm). The staff speak English, but their helpfulness varies enormously; however, they can usually answer most enquiries, and can organize accommodation, and sell maps, guides and theatre tickets.

The best **website** for finding your way around the capital is ⓦwww.mapy .cz, which will help you locate any hotel, restaurant, pub, shop or street in Prague. A more general, informative site is Radio Prague's ⓦwww.radio.cz /english, which includes the latest news. For information on what's happening in Prague as well as other suggestions for things to see and do, check the website ⓦwww.expats.cz.

Festivals and events

EPIPHANY (TŘÍ KRÁLOVÉ)

January 6
The letters K + M + B followed by the date of the new year are chalked on doorways across the capital to celebrate the "Day of the Three Kings" when the Magi came to worship Christ.

MASOPUST OR CARNEVALE

Shrove Tuesday
The approach of Masopust (the Czech version of Mardi Gras) is celebrated locally in the Žižkov district of Prague, where there's a five-day programme of parties, concerts and parades; a more mainstream series of events takes place under the umbrella of Carnevale, in the city centre.

EASTER (VELIKONOCE)

The age-old sexist ritual of whipping girls' calves with braided birch twigs tied together with ribbons (*pomlázky*) is still practised outside of Prague. To prevent such a fate, the girls are supposed to offer the boys a coloured Easter egg and pour a bucket of cold water over them. You'll see *pomlázky* and Easter eggs on sale, but precious little whipping.

DAYS OF EUROPEAN FILM (DNY EVROPSKÉHO FILMU)

April Ⓦ www.eurofilmfest.cz
This is the nearest Prague comes to a film festival: a fortnight of arty European films shown at various screens across the capital.

"BURNING OF THE WITCHES" (PÁLENÍ ČARODĚJNIC)

April 30
Halloween comes early to the Czech Republic when bonfires are lit across the country, and old brooms thrown out and burned, as everyone celebrates the end of the long winter.

PRAGUE INTERNATIONAL MARATHON

Early May Ⓦ www.runczech.com.
Runners from over fifty countries come to race through the city's cobbled streets and over Charles Bridge.

PRAGUE SPRING FESTIVAL (PRAŽSKÉ JARO)

May 12–June 2 Box office at Obecní dům, Náměstí Republiky 5, ☎ 257 312 547, Ⓦ www .festival.cz.
By far the biggest annual arts event and the country's most prestigious international music festival. Established in 1946, it traditionally begins on May 12, the anniversary of Smetana's death, with a procession from his grave in Vyšehrad to the Obecní dům where the composer's *Má vlast* (My Country) is performed in the presence of the president, finishing on June 2 with a rendition of Beethoven's *Ninth Symphony*. Tickets for the festival sell out fast – they are typically made available online in December.

WORLD ROMA FESTIVAL (KHAMORO)

Late May Ⓦ www.khamoro.cz.
International Roma festival of music, dance and film, plus seminars and workshops.

PRAGUE FRINGE FESTIVAL

Late May/early June Ⓦ www.praguefringe.com.

Your best chance to see English-language theatre in Prague, and good stuff at that. Organizers pack in the shows, and venues are all conveniently located in Malá Strana.

DANCE PRAGUE (TANEC PRAHA)

Four weeks in late May–late June
Ⓦ www.tanecpraha.cz

An established highlight of Prague's cultural calendar, this international festival of modern dance takes place at venues throughout the city.

RESPECT FESTIVAL

June Ⓦ www.respectfestival.rachot.cz.

This world music weekend is held at various venues across the city in June, including the Akropolis and Štvanice island.

BURČÁK

September

For a couple of weeks, stalls on street corners sell the year's partially fermented new wine, known as *burčák*, a misty, heady brew.

STRINGS OF AUTUMN

Late September–early November
Ⓦ www.strunypodzimu.cz.

Excellent line-up of local and international orchestras and musicians from a wide range of genres. Tickets for this creative festival held in interesting venues go fast.

CHRISTMAS MARKETS

Christmas markets selling gifts, food and mulled wine (*svářák*) are set up at several places around the city in

Public holidays

January 1 New Year's Day; **Easter Monday**; **May 1** May Day; **May 8** VE Day; **July 5** SS Cyril and Methodius Day; **July 6** Jan Hus Day; **September 28** St Wenceslas Day; **October 28** Foundation of the Republic; **November 17** Battle for Freedom and Democracy Day; **December 24** Christmas Eve; **December 25** Christmas Day; **December 26** St Stephen's Day

December: the biggest ones are on Wenceslas Square and the Old Town Square. Temporary ice rinks are also constructed at various locations.

EVE OF ST NICHOLAS

December 5

On the evening of December 5, numerous trios, dressed up as St Nicholas (svatý Mikuláš), an angel and a devil, tour round the streets, the angel handing out sweets and fruit to children who've been good, while the devil dishes out coal and potatoes to those who've been naughty. The Czech St Nicholas has white hair and a beard, and dresses not in red but in a white priest's outfit, with a bishop's mitre.

CHRISTMAS EVE (ŠTĚDRÝ VEČER)

December 24 is traditionally a day of fasting, broken only when the evening star appears, signalling the beginning of the Christmas feast of carp, potato salad, schnitzel and sweetbreads. Only after the meal are the children allowed to open their presents, which miraculously appear beneath the tree, thanks not to Santa Claus, but to Baby Jesus (Ježíšek).

Chronology

895 > First recorded Přemyslid duke and first Christian ruler of Prague, Bořivoj, baptized by saints Cyril and Methodius.

929 > Prince Václav ("Good King Wenceslas") is martyred by his pagan brother Boleslav the Cruel.

973 > Under Boleslav the Pious, Prague becomes a bishopric.

1212 > Otakar I secures a royal title for himself and his descendants, who thereafter become kings of Bohemia.

1305 > Václav II dies heirless, ending the Přemyslid dynasty.

1346–78 > During the reign of Holy Roman Emperor Charles IV, Prague enjoys its first Golden Age as the city is transformed by building projects into a fitting imperial capital.

1389 > Three thousand Jews slaughtered in the worst pogrom of the medieval period.

1415 > Czech religious reformer Jan Hus is found guilty of heresy and burnt at the stake in Konstanz (Constance).

1419 > Prague's first defenestration. Hus's followers, known as the Hussites, throw several councillors to their deaths from the windows of Prague's Nové Město's town hall.

1420 > Battle of Vítkov (a hill in Prague). Jan Žižka leads the Hussites to victory over papal forces.

1434 > Battle of Lipany. The radical Hussites are defeated by an army of moderates and Catholics.

1526 > Habsburg rule in Prague begins, as Emperor Ferdinand I is elected King of Bohemia.

1576–1611 > Emperor Rudolf II establishes Prague as the royal seat of power, and ushers in the city's second Golden Age, summoning artists, astronomers and alchemists from all of Europe.

1618 > Prague's second defenestration. Two Catholic governors are thrown from the windows of Prague Castle by Bohemian Protestants. The Thirty Years' War begins.

1620 > Battle of the White Mountain, just outside Prague. The Protestants, under the "Winter King" Frederick of the Palatinate, are defeated by the Catholic forces; 27 Protestant nobles are executed on the Old Town Square.

1648 > The (Protestant) Swedes are defeated on Charles Bridge by Prague's Jewish and student populations. The Thirty Years' War ends.

1713 > Plague kills 13,000.

1757 > During the Seven Years' War, Prague is besieged and bombarded by the Prussians.

1781 > Edict of Tolerance issued by Emperor Joseph II, allowing a large degree of freedom of worship for the first time in 150 years.

1848 > Uprising in Prague eventually put down by Habsburg commander Alfred Prince

Windischgätz. The ensuing reforms allow Jews to settle outside the ghetto for the first time.

1918 > The Habsburg Empire collapses due to defeat in World War I. Czechoslovakia founded.

1920 > Tomáš Masaryk elected as first president of Czechoslovakia.

1935 > Edvard Beneš elected as the second president of Czechoslovakia.

1938 > According to the Munich Agreement drawn up by Britain, France, Fascist Italy and Nazi Germany, the Czechs are forced to secede the border regions of the Sudetenland to Hitler.

1939 > In March, the Germans invade and occupy the rest of the Czech Lands. Slovakia declares independence.

1941 > Prague's Jews deported to Terezín (Theresienstadt) before being sent to the concentration camps.

1942 > Nazi leader Reinhard Heydrich assassinated in Prague. The villages of Lidice and Ležáky are annihilated in retaliation.

1945 > On May 5, the Prague Uprising against the Nazis begins. On May 9, the Russians liberate the city. The city's ethnic German population is brutally expelled.

1946 > Communist Party wins up to forty percent of the vote in first postwar general election. Beneš formally re-elected as president.

1948 > The Communist Party seizes power in a bloodless coup in February. Thousands flee the country. Jan Masaryk, Foreign Minister and son of the former president, dies in mysterious circumstances. Beneš resigns as president, replaced by Communist leader, Klement Gottwald.

1952 > Twelve leading Party members (eleven of them Jewish) sentenced to death as traitors in Prague's infamous show trials.

1953 > Gottwald dies five days after Stalin.

1968 > During the "Prague Spring", reformers within the Party abolish censorship. Soviet troops invade and stop the reform movement. Thousands go into exile.

1977 > 243 Czechs and Slovaks, including playwright Václav Havel, sign Charter 77 manifesto, reigniting the dissident movement.

1989 > After two weeks of popular protest, known as the Velvet Revolution, the Communist government resigns. Havel is elected as president.

1993 > Czechoslovakia splits into the Czech Republic and Slovakia. Havel is elected as Czech president.

1999 > The Czech Republic joins NATO.

2002 > In August, Prague is devastated by the worst floods in 200 years.

2003 > Václav Klaus is elected as the second Czech president.

2004 > The Czech Republic enters the European Union.

2013 > Czechs elect Miloš Zeman in the country's first direct presidential election.

Czech

A modicum of English is spoken in Prague's central restaurants and hotels, and among the city's younger generation. Any attempt to speak Czech will be heartily appreciated, though don't be discouraged if people seem not to understand, as most will be unaccustomed to hearing foreigners stumble through their language. Unfortunately, Czech (**český**) is a highly complex western Slav tongue, into which you're unlikely to make much headway during a short stay.

Pronunciation

English-speakers often find Czech impossibly difficult to pronounce: just try the Czech tongue-twister, strč prst skrz krk (stick your finger down your neck). The good news is that, apart from a few special letters, each letter and syllable is pronounced as it's written – the trick is always to stress the first syllable of a word, no matter what its length; otherwise you'll render it unintelligible.

SHORT AND LONG VOWELS

Czech has both short and long vowels (the latter being denoted by a variety of accents):

a like the u in cup
á as in father
e as in pet
é as in fair
ě like the ye in yes
i or y as in pit
í or ý as in seat
o as in not
ó as in door
u like the oo in book
ů or ú like the oo in fool

VOWEL COMBINATIONS AND DIPHTHONGS

There are very few diphthongs in Czech, so any combinations of vowels other than those below should be pronounced as two separate syllables.

au like the ou in foul
ou like the oe in foe

CONSONANTS AND ACCENTS

There are no silent consonants, but it's worth remembering that r and l can form a half-syllable if standing between two other consonants or at the end of a word, as in Brno (Br-no) or Vltava (Vl-ta-va). The consonants listed below are those which differ substantially from the English. Accents look daunting, particularly the háček, which appears above c, d, n, r, s, t and z, but the only one which causes a lot of problems is ř, probably the most difficult letter to say in the entire language – even Czech toddlers have to be taught how to say it.

c like the ts in boats
č like the ch in chicken
ch like the ch in the Scottish loch
ď like the d in duped

The alphabet

In the Czech alphabet, letters which feature a **háček** (as in the č of the word itself) are considered separate letters and appear in Czech indexes immediately after their more familiar cousins. More confusingly, the consonant combination ch is also considered as a separate letter and appears in Czech indexes after the letter h.

g always as in goat, never as in general

h always as in have, but more energetic

j like the **y** in yoke

kd pronounced as **gd**

mě pronounced as mnye

ñ like the **n** in nuance

p softer than the English **p**

r as in rip, but often rolled

ř approximately like the sound of **r** and **ž** combined

š like the **sh** in shop

tʼ like the **t** in tutor

ž like the **s** in pleasure; at the end of a word like the **sh** in shop

Words and phrases

BASICS

Yes	ano
No	ne
Please/excuse me	prosím vás
Don't mention it	není zač
Sorry	pardon
Thank you	děkuju
Bon appétit	dobrou chuť
Bon voyage	šťastnou cestu
Hello/goodbye (informal)	ahoj
Hello (formal)	dobrý den
Goodbye (formal)	na shledanou
Good morning	dobré ráno
Good evening	dobrý večer
Good night (when leaving)	dobrou noc
How are you?	jak se máte?
I'm English/Irish /Scottish /Welsh /American	ja jsem angličan(ka)/ ir(ka)/skot(ka)/ velšan(ka)/ američan(ka)
Do you speak English?	mluvíte anglicky?
I don't speak German	nemluvím německy
I don't understand	nerozumím
I understand	rozumím
I don't know	nevím
Speak slowly	mluvte pomalu
How do you say that in Czech?	jak se to řekne česky?
Could you write it down for me?	mužete mi to napsat?

Today	dnes
Yesterday	včera
Tomorrow	zítra
The day after tomorrow	pozítří
Now	hned
Later	později
Wait a minute!	moment
Leave me alone!	dej mi pokoj!
Go away!	jdi pryč!
Help!	pomoc!
This one	toto
A little	trochu
Another one	ještě jedno
Large/small	velký/malý
More/less	více/méně
Good/bad	dobrý/špatný
Cheap/expensive	levný/drahý
Hot/cold	horký/studený
With/without	s/bez
The bill please	zaplatím prosím
Do you have ...?	máte ...?
We don't have	nemáme
We do have	máme

QUESTIONS

What?	co?
Where?	kde?
When?	kdy?
Why?	proč?
Which one?	který/ktera/které?
This one?	ten/ta/to?
How many?	kolik?
What time does it open?	kdy máte otevřeno?
What time does it close?	kdy zavíráte?

GETTING AROUND

Over here	tady
Over there	tam
Left	nalevo
Right	napravo
Straight on	rovně
Where is ...?	kde je ...?
How do I get to Prague?	jak se dostanu do Prahy ?
How do I get to the...?	jak se dostanu k...?

147

By bus	autobusem
By train	vlakem
By car	autem
On foot	pěšky
By taxi	taxíkem
Stop here, please	zastavte tady, prosím
Ticket	jízdenka/lístek
Return ticket	zpáteční
Train station	nádraží
Bus station	autobusové nádraží
Bus stop	autobusová zastávka
When's the next train to Prague?	kdy jede další vlak do Prahy?
Is it going to Prague?	jede to do Prahy?
Do I have to change?	musím přestupovat?
Do I need a reservation?	musím mít místenku?
Is this seat free?	je tu volno?
May we (sit down)?	můžeme (se sednout)?

ACCOMMODATION

Are there any rooms available?	máte volné pokoje?
Do you have a double room?	máte jednou dvou lůžkovy pokoj?
For one night	na jednu noc
With shower	se sprchou
With bath	s koupelnou
How much is it?	kolík to stojí?
With breakfast?	se snídaní?

SOME SIGNS

Entrance	vchod
Exit	východ
Toilets	záchody/toalety
Men	muži
Women	ženy
Ladies	dámy
Gentlemen	pánové
Open	otevřeno
Closed	zavřeno
Pull/Push	sem/tam
Danger!	pozor!
Hospital	nemocnice
No smoking	kouření zakázáno
No entry	vstup zakázán

Arrival	příjezd
Departure	odjezd

DAYS OF THE WEEK

Monday	pondělí
Tuesday	uterý
Wednesday	středa
Thursday	čtvrtek
Friday	pátek
Saturday	sobota
Sunday	neděle
Day	den
Week	týden
Month	měsíc
Year	rok

MONTHS OF THE YEAR

Many Slav languages have their own highly individual systems in which the words for the names of the months are descriptive nouns, sometimes beautifully apt for the month in question.

January	leden (ice)
February	únor (hibernation)
March	březen (birch)
April	duben (oak)
May	květen (blossom)
June	červen (red)
July	červenec (red)
August	srpen (sickle)
September	zaří (blazing)
October	říjen (rutting)
November	listopad (leaves falling)
December	prosinec (millet porridge)

NUMBERS

1	jeden
2	dva
3	tří
4	čtyři
5	pět
6	šest
7	sedm
8	osm
9	devět
10	deset

11	jedenáct
12	dvanáct
13	třináct
14	čtrnáct
15	patnáct
16	šestnáct
17	sedmnáct
18	osmnáct
19	devatenáct
20	dvacet
21	dvacetjedna
30	třicet
40	čtyřicet
50	padesát
60	šedesát
70	sedmdesát
80	osmdesát
90	devadesát
100	sto
101	sto jedna
155	sto padesát pět
200	dvě stě
300	tři sta
400	čtyři sta
500	pět set
600	šest set
700	sedm set
800	osm set
900	devět set
1000	tisíc

Food and drink terms
BASICS

chléb	bread
chlebíček	(open) sandwich
cukr	sugar
hořčice	mustard
houska	round roll
knedlíky	dumplings
křen	horseradish
lžíce	spoon
maso	meat
máslo	butter
med	honey
mléko	milk
moučník	dessert
nápoje	drinks
na zdraví	cheers!
nůž	knife

oběd	lunch
obloha	garnish
ocet	vinegar
ovoce	fruit
pečivo	rolls
pepř	pepper
polévka	soup
předkrmy	starters
přílohy	side dishes
rohlík	finger roll
ryby	fish
rýže	rice
sklenice	glass
snídaně	breakfast
sůl	salt
šálek	cup
talíř	plate
tartarská omáčka	tartare sauce
večeře	supper/dinner
vejce	eggs
vidlička	fork
volské oko	fried egg
zeleniny	vegetables

COMMON TERMS

čerstvý	fresh
domácí	home-made
dušený	stew/casserole
grilovaný	roast on the spit
kyselý	sour
na kmíně	with caraway seeds
na roštu	grilled
nadívaný	stuffed
nakládaný	pickled
(za)pečený	baked/roast
plněný	stuffed
s máslem	with butter
sladký	sweet
slaný	salted
smažený	fried in breadcrumbs
studený	cold
syrový	raw
sýrový	cheesy
teplý	hot
uzený	smoked
vařený	boiled

SOUPS

boršč	beetroot soup
bramborová	potato soup
čočková	lentil soup
fazolová	bean soup
hovězí vývar	beef broth
hrachová	pea soup
kuřecí	thin chicken soup
rajská	tomato soup
zeleninová	vegetable soup

FISH

kapr	carp
losos	salmon
makrela	mackerel
platys	flounder
pstruh	trout
rybí filé	fillet of fish
sardinka	sardine
štika	pike
treska	cod
zavináč	herring/rollmop

MEAT DISHES

bažant	pheasant
biftek	beef steak
čevapčiči	spicy meatballs
dršťky	tripe
drůbež	poultry
guláš	goulash
hovězí	beef
husa	goose
játra	liver
jazyk	tongue
kachna	duck
klobásy	sausages
kotleta	cutlet
kuře	chicken
kýta	leg
ledvinky	kidneys
řízek	steak
roštěná	sirloin
salám	salami
sekaná	meat loaf
skopové maso	mutton
slanina	bacon
svíčková	fillet of beef

šunka	ham
telecí	veal
vepřový	pork
vepřové řízek	breaded pork cutlet or schnitzel
zajíc	hare
žebírko	ribs

VEGETABLES

brambory	potatoes
brokolice	broccoli
celer	celery
cibule	onion
česnek	garlic
chřest	asparagus
čočka	lentils
fazole	beans
houby	mushrooms
hranolky	chips, French fries
hrášek	peas
karot	carrot
květák	cauliflower
kyselá okurka	pickled gherkin
kyselé zelí	sauerkraut
lečo	ratatouille
lilek	aubergine
okurka	cucumber
pórek	leek
rajče	tomato
ředkev	radish
řepná bulva	beetroot
špenát	spinach
zelí	cabbage
žampiony	mushrooms

FRUIT, CHEESE AND NUTS

arašídy	peanuts
banán	banana
borůvky	blueberries
broskev	peach
brusinky	cranberries
bryndza	goat's cheese in brine
citrón	lemon
grep	grapefruit
hermelín	Czech brie
hrozny	grapes
hruška	pear

jablko	apple
jahody	strawberries
kompot	stewed fruit
maliny	raspberries
mandle	almonds
meruňka	apricot
niva	semi-soft, crumbly, blue cheese
ostružiny	blackberries
oštěpek	heavily smoked, curd cheese
pivní sýr	cheese flavoured with beer
pomeranč	orange
rozinky	raisins
švestky	plums
třešně	cherries
tvaroh	fresh curd cheese
uzený sýr	smoked cheese
vlašské ořechy	walnuts

DRINKS

čaj	tea
destiláty	spirits
káva	coffee
koňak	brandy
láhev	bottle
minerální (voda)	mineral (water)
mléko	milk
pivo	beer
presso	espresso
s ledem	with ice
soda	soda
suché víno	dry wine
šumivý	fizzy
svařené víno /svařák	mulled wine
tonic	tonic
vinný střik	white wine with soda
víno	wine

A glossary of Czech terms

brána	gate
český	Bohemian
chrám	cathedral
divadlo	theatre
dům	house
hora	mountain
hospoda /hostinec	pub
hrad	castle
hřbitov	cemetery
kaple	chapel
katedrála	cathedral
kavárna	coffee house
klášter	monastery/convent
kostel	church
koupaliště	swimming pool
Labe	River Elbe
lanovka	funicular/cable car
les	forest
město	town
most	bridge
muzeum	museum
nábřeží	embankment
nádraží	train station
náměstí	square
ostrov	island
palác	palace
památník	memorial or monument
pasáž	interior shopping arcade
pivnice	pub
radnice	town hall
restaurace	restaurant
sad	park
sál	room or hall
schody	steps
svatý/svatá	saint; often abbreviated to sv
třída	avenue
ulice	street
věž	tower
vinárna	wine bar or cellar
Vltava	River Moldau
vrchy	hills
výstava	exhibition
zahrada	garden
zámek	chateau

PUBLISHING INFORMATION

This third edition published September 2016 by **Rough Guides Ltd**

80 Strand, London WC2R 0RL

11, Community Centre, Panchsheel Park, New Delhi 110017, India

Distributed by Penguin Random House

Penguin Books Ltd, 80 Strand, London WC2R 0RL

Penguin Group (USA) 345 Hudson Street, NY 10014, USA

Penguin Group (Australia) 250 Camberwell Road, Camberwell, Victoria 3124, Australia

Penguin Group (NZ) 67 Apollo Drive, Mairangi Bay, Auckland 1310, New Zealand

Penguin Group (South Africa) Block D, Rosebank Office Park, 181 Jan Smuts Avenue,

Parktown North, Gauteng, South Africa 2193

Rough Guides is represented in Canada by

DK Canada 320 Front Street West, Suite 1400, Toronto, Ontario M5V 3B6

Typeset in Minion and Din to an original design by Henry Iles and Dan May.

Printed and bound in China

© Rough Guides 2016

Maps © Rough Guides

160pp includes index

A catalogue record for this book is available from the British Library

ISBN 978-0-24124-916-1

MIX
Paper from
responsible sources
FSC™ C018179

ROUGH GUIDES CREDITS

Editor: Olivia Rawes

Layout: Anita Singh

Cartography: Ed Wright

Picture editor: Michelle Bhatia

Photographers: Natascha Sturny, Dan Bannister and Eddie Gerald

Proofreader: Jan McCann

Managing editor: Monica Woods

Production: Jimmy Lao

Cover photo research: Nicole Newman

Editorial assistant: Freya Godfrey

Senior DTP coordinator: Dan May

Publishing director: Georgina Dee

THE AUTHOR

Marc Di Duca has been a full-time travel guide author for the past decade, covering destinations as diverse as Madeira and Siberia for most major travel publishers. Marc is a fluent Czech speaker and has lived, worked and played in the country on and off for the past 25 years. As well as penning guides he also works as a translator for CzechTourism and Prague-based COT Media.

HELP US UPDATE

We've gone to a lot of effort to ensure that the first edition of the **Pocket Rough Guide Prague** is accurate and up-to-date. However, things change – places get "discovered", opening hours are notoriously fickle, restaurants and rooms raise prices or lower standards. If you feel we've got it wrong or left something out, we'd like to know, and if you can remember the address, the price, the hours, the phone number, so much the better.

Please send your comments with the subject line "**Pocket Rough Guide Prague Update**" to mail@roughguides.com. We'll credit all contributions and send a copy of the next edition (or any other Rough Guide if you prefer) for the very best emails.

Find more travel information, connect with fellow travellers and book your trip on roughguides.com

PHOTO CREDITS

All photos © Rough Guides except the following:
(Key: t-top; c-centre; b-bottom; l-left; r-right)

1 Dreamstime.com: Lindrik
2 4Corners: SIME / Pietro Canali
5 Alamy Stock Photo: Eric Nathan
9 Ambiente (b)
11 Alamy Stock Photo: Profimedia.CZ a.s. (b)
12 4Corners: SIME / Pietro Canali
23 DOX (br). **Museum Kam** (bl)
24 Dreamstime.com: Darellian
37 Alamy Stock Photo: Profimedia.CZ a.s.
61 Dreamstime.com: Vitaly Titov & Maria Sidelnikova
69 SuperStock: Peter Erik Forsberg
71 Naprstek museum
85 Alamy Stock Photo: Yadid Levy
86 Dreamstime.com: Singhsomendra
87 Dreamstime.com: Tomas Pisek
94 Ambiente

101 Alamy Stock Photo: Peter Erik Forsberg
105 Dynamo
110 Alamy Stock Photo: Profimedia.CZ a.s.
115 Alamy Stock Photo: Peter Forsberg
117 Alamy Stock Photo: CTK
118 Dreamstime.com: Mirekdeml
124 Zoo Praha: Tomáš Adamec
126–127 Hotel Paris: Filip Obr
134–135 Dreamstime.com: David Pereiras Villagrá

Front cover and spine: *Charles Bridge at dawn*
Corbis: Rob Tilley

Back cover: *Wallenstein Palace and the Castle Garden* **Alamy Stock Photo:** imageBROKER / Martin Moxter

Index

Maps are marked in **bold**

157

SO NOW WE'VE TOLD YOU
ABOUT THE THINGS NOT TO
MISS, THE BEST PLACES TO
STAY, THE TOP RESTAURANTS,
THE LIVELIEST BARS AND THE
MOST SPECTACULAR SIGHTS,
IT ONLY SEEMS FAIR TO
TELL YOU ABOUT THE BEST
TRAVEL INSURANCE AROUND